Other titles in the series

Series Editors: William and Carol Rohwer
University of California, Berkeley

Learner Differences: Diagnosis and Prescription

Learner Differences: Diagnosis and Prescription

Joel R. Levin
University of Wisconsin

Holt, Rinehart and Winston
New York, Chicago, San Francisco, Atlanta,
Montreal, Toronto, London, Sydney, Dallas

To Sonia and Norman, Ida and Michael

Library of Congress Cataloging in Publication Data

Levin, Joel R.
  Learner differences.

  (Principles of educational psychology series)
  Includes bibliographical references.
  1. Learning, Psychology of.   I. Title.
LB1051.L597   370.15′2   76-46364
ISBN 0-03-015296-8

Foreword

The Principles of Educational Psychology Series

The materials used to present educational psychology to
teachers should have two dominant characteristics—
excellence and adaptability. The *Principles of Educational
Psychology Series* aspires to both. It consists of several
short books, each devoted to an essential topic in the field.
The authors of the books are responsible for their excellence; each author is noted for a command of his or her
topic and for a deep conviction of the importance of the
topic for teachers. Taken as a whole, the series provides
comprehensive coverage of the major topics in educational
psychology, but it is by no means a survey, for every topic
is illuminated in a distinctive way by the individual approach of each author.

Numerous considerations require that the materials used

for instruction in educational psychology be adaptable. One consideration is that the readership is heterogeneous, including students in pre-service teacher training programs, of whom some have and others have not taken prior work in psychology, as well as professional teachers in in-service programs who have already completed previous courses in educational psychology. The separate booklets in the *Principles of Educational Psychology Series* are intended to be responsive to these differences. The writing is clear and direct, providing easy access for the novice, and the authors' fresh and distinctive viewpoints offer new insights to the more experienced.

Another consideration is that the format of courses in educational psychology varies widely. A course may be designed for pre-service or for in-service programs, for early childhood, elementary, secondary, or comprehensive programs, or to offer special preparation for teaching in urban, suburban, or rural settings. The course may occupy a full academic year, a semester, trimester, quarter, or an even shorter period. A common set of topics may be offered to all students in the course, or the topical coverage may be individualized. The *Principles of Educational Psychology Series* can be adapted to any one of these formats. Since the series consists of separate books, each one treating a single topic, instructors and students can choose to adopt the entire set or selected volumes from it, depending on the length, topical emphasis, and structure of the course.

The need for effective means of training teachers is of increasing urgency. To assist in meeting that need, the intent of the series is to provide materials for presenting educational psychology that are distinctive in approach, excellent in execution, and adaptable in use.

William Rohwer
Carol Rohwer
Series Editors
Berkeley, California
February, 1974

Preface

This book is about learners. More specifically, it is about the characteristics of individuals who learn; how to recognize similarities and differences among them; and given this information, what we, as educators can do. Though much of our discussion depends on the general laws and principles of *learning*, we are more concerned here with the *learners* themselves. (For an examination of learning processes in children, see the Reese, 1976, and Gagné, 1974, volumes in this series.)

Chapter 1 provides an introduction to the diagnosis-prescription orientation of this book. I have included in this first chapter some of my own beliefs and biases about the educator's role in recognizing and dealing with various learner characteristics. Chapter 2 presents some basic concepts from the field of educational measurement that will enable us to pursue questions of learner differences from a technical, yet intuitive, standpoint. We will use these concepts to develop a model for diagnosing learner differences and prescribing instructional treatments to deal with them. Chapter 3 concentrates on the diagnosis side of this model, and Chapter 4 examines the prescription side. We conclude in Chapter 5 with an example of how a classroom teacher might implement the various components of the model presented.

The book was put together with the help of some special individuals. I am particularly grateful to Connie Shelhamer, who types impeccably; to Bill and Carol Rohwer and to Jackie Pourciau, whose editorial suggestions greatly enhanced the character and readability of the book; to Tom Kratochwill and Mike Subkoviak, for thoughtful comments on an earlier draft; and, above all, to Barbara Levin, educator *par excellence* and the one who *really* knows

"where it's at." And of course to 🙁 and 🙂 —how

could I ever forget? Without folks like you, there would be no learner differences to speak of.

Joel R. Levin
Madison, Wisconsin
January 1977

Contents

Contents

Learner Differences: Diagnosis and Prescription

Chapter 1 Introduction

Chapter 1   Introduction

This book is about learners and, in particular, differences among learners. In considering learner differences, we will be concerned with (1) what such differences are and what they imply, and, (2) having done this, how to deal with them. Clearly, questions of *what* have been considered extensively in the past. (For a sampling, refer to almost any introductory textbook in the field of differential psychology, e.g., Anastasi, 1958; Tyler, 1965; as well as to recent educationally oriented books, e.g., Brophy and Good, 1974; Lesser, 1971b.) Because of this, the material to be presented here is not intended to be an exhaustive rehash of that content. Rather, we will develop a rationale for considering learner differences, along with some strategies for dealing with learner differences and some manifestations of these strategies in current educational programs.

As we proceed through the book, we shall frequently be making comparisons among different learners. Whenever comparisons of this kind are made, you will do well to keep in mind two things. First, even though two learners may seem to be similar in some or most respects, this does not imply that they are exactly alike in those respects. Nor does it imply that they are similar in all of them. Second, recognizing similarities among learners can be extremely important when it comes to deciding how to deal with individuals in the classroom. Let us consider each of these in turn.

The notion that two individuals may be similar in some respects but not identical in all is nicely illustrated by Kagan, Moss, and Sigel (1963). These authors contrast the play activity of two three-and-a-half-year-old boys, both of whom had been attending the same nursery school for six months. One of the children (B):

. . . flitted from one activity to another. He worked puzzles, looked at books with one of the observers, joined the girls for a tea party for a moment, or dashed off a painting. Out of doors he rode a tricycle and bumped into the girls. On the jungle gym he would rock wildly with the boys. He constantly approached the teacher for attention and called the teacher if he was losing a fight. B rarely played alone and usually tried to dominate the other children. He occasionally made the girls cry by hitting or pushing them [p. 106].

On the other hand, the second child (A):

. . . usually played quiet sedentary games, rarely

joined in the wild running or shouting. He frequently sat by himself and played contentedly, talking to himself as he looked at a book or arranged the dishes. He put puzzles together and fitted train tracks in a neat row. He seemed to enjoy coloring with a group of children and often joined peers at the craft table. When fitting the tracks together or working on a puzzle alone, he usually ignored everything else in the room. Sometimes he played in a corner with his back to the room or sang and talked quietly to himself while putting his teddy bear to bed. (Child) A was never observed to interfere with another child's play or to make an unprovoked attack, and he often allowed other children to take his toys without objecting [p. 106].

These passages reveal the dramatically different play patterns of two children. Child B tends to be active and aggressive in his play while Child A tends to be passive and solitary. Surely this comes as no surprise to you, who have likely encountered many children at both extremes of the active-passive continuum. Even the fact that these different social behaviors are exhibited by two children of the same age and sex and with the same amount of nursery school exposure is not startling. Something else should be pointed out, however. These two boys were also of the same intelligence and came from the same family background. But would it startle you to learn that A and B were fraternal twins? Well they were. Thus, despite the vast number of similar characteristics that could be attributed to these two children, marked differences in their typical play styles are still apparent.

Our second point—that similarities are valuable in their own right—is evidenced by the doctor who prescribes the same medicine or treatment for different patients with similar symptoms. Even though the doctor is well aware that different patients do not exhibit precisely the same symptoms (or, for that matter, that the same drug will not have precisely the same effect on different individuals with similar symptoms), his prescriptions are based on previous—and presumably successful—prescriptive experiences with patients exhibiting similar symptoms. Clearly the assumption underlying this philosophy is that it is possible to classify or group patients on the basis of similar symptoms and that useful prescriptions can then be made on the basis of these general symptom classifications.

The similar symptom philosophy of the medical profession leaves little to chance, inasmuch as the drugs and treatments prescribed have been thoroughly tested for their effectiveness and carefully screened to assure that adverse reactions are unlikely. However, in other contexts, decisions relating to individuals can only be framed in terms of *probabilities of success*. Thus, if you happen to be a 35-year-old green-eyed mortician from Timbuctoo who "digs" Lawrence Welk and who drives 37½ miles to work every evening in a 1949 polka-dotted convertible hearse, the Fly By Night Insurance Company may charge you a premium based on carefully calculated "accident probabilities" for people like yourself. In determining the amount of your premium, Fly By Night will not be able to state with certainty how much you as an individual will cost the company—especially since yours is a hearse of a different color! However, considering previous data on individuals of *similar* ages in *similar* occupations (e.g., chauffeurs, archeologists, and professors) who drive *similar* distances to work in *similar* vehicles, Fly By Night assigns a premium which reflects how much people *like you* have cost the company in the past.

As we shall see in Chapter 4, given the current state of the art, most prescriptions in education must also be made in terms of probability statements. That is, as teachers we can be aware of particular instructional methods and curricular materials that in the past have tended to work well for students with certain characteristics. But there is no guarantee that they will, in fact, work for a particular student with those characteristics. Nonetheless, the most reasonable solution is to prescribe for that student the methods and materials that have the *highest probability of success* (as determined from previous experience), rather than to operate indiscriminately.

To summarize, the fact that people differ is no great revelation; ask any shoe manufacturer. However, shoe manufacturers have recognized and responded to the differences among shoe-wearers, while the same cannot be said for the guardians of our educational institutions and, in particular, teachers. Even though teachers may at times exhibit an awareness of student differences in their classrooms, this awareness is rarely reflected in their teaching behaviors. Too often a "one class, one teaching method" philosophy prevails in the classroom, a philosophy that cannot be responsive to the tremendous diversity represented by the students therein. Fortunately this dormant period in education is giving way to a period of awakening, to the point where, as Gerald Lesser (1971b) has put it, "Recognizing and respecting the individual differences among children now has become one of education's most cherished chestnuts [p. 7]." Hopefully you will be able to chew on some of these chestnuts in the remaining chapters.

Suggested Readings

Brophy, J. E., & Good, T. L. *Teacher-student relationships: Causes and consequences.* New York: Holt, Rinehart and Winston, 1974.

Lesser, G. S. (Ed.) *Psychology and educational practice.* Glenview, Ill.: Scott, Foresman, 1971b.

Chapter 2   Differences as Variation

The story of learner differences begins with the study of *variability* or *variation*. The concept of variation has the same connotative meaning in psychology as it does in our daily lives. Just as there is variation in the performance of the same make automobile or in the culinary products of two cooks following the same recipe or simply in the pattern of weather from one day to the next (at least in the midwest), so, too, there is variation in almost every measured characteristic of learners. Because variation is inherent in learner characteristics, these characteristics are commonly referred to as learner *variables*.

Input versus Output Variables

Let us assume that the major function of schooling is for the student to learn something, whether it be curricular material, basic technical skills, citizenship, personal and emotional adjustment, crocheting, or simply how to think logically. We will refer to these learning outcomes (i.e., outcomes of schooling and instruction) as *output* variables. On the other hand, those traits, abilities, and prerequisites that students bring with them into the learning environment will be termed *input* variables. Input and output variables make up the two general classes of learner variables operative in school-learning situations.

Input variables include height, weight, age, blood type, birthplace, sex, income level, and similar census-type information that serves to identify individuals. Such variables tend to be either measurable (e.g., height in inches, age in months, annual income in dollars) or at least specifiable (e.g., birthplace in terms of a particular city or state and blood type and sex in terms of biological, chemical, and anatomical indices). In addition to these *identification* variables, input variables also include psychological traits, which are not as easily measured or defined but which can be inferred from an individual's behavior. Accordingly, these variables are known as *behavioral* variables.

Thus, a student who produces an unusual painting is labeled "creative" by his teacher; a student who appears to be trying hard in school is "motivated"; and one whom the teacher finds hard to discipline is "disruptive." With behavioral variables it is important to realize that (1) the reality of the construct is intimately tied to our interpretation of a behavior, and (2) since the ability to assess a particular behavior varies, the same behavior may be interpreted quite differently by different observers or by the same observer on different occasions. Such issues form the basis of *psychometric theory* or the theory of psychological measurement (Green, forthcoming; Stanley and Hopkins, 1972; Lyman, 1971).

Output variables include all outcomes of schooling (such as those listed earlier) that typically differentiate among students with respect to *what* and *how much* is learned, that is, with respect to the variety of educational outcomes achieved and their degree of mastery. Most output variables tend to be of the behavioral variety in that the unseen achievement outcomes that we attribute to students are almost always inferred on the basis of behavior samples (including test performances). Consider, for example, the evidence on which we base our conclusions concerning a particular student's knowledge of fractions, typing ability, or crocheting prowess.

Kinds of Variation

Interindividual Variation

The common sense notion that no two snowflakes (or people) are exactly alike gets at the heart of interindividual variation. Thus, upon identifying a behavioral output variable such as reading achievement, it is possible to identify students whose performances associated with that variable are different. For example, within a classroom we can identify a child whose reading achievement score on a standardized test such as the Stanford Achievement Test is low, another whose score is high, and so forth, such that we can obtain a *distribution* of

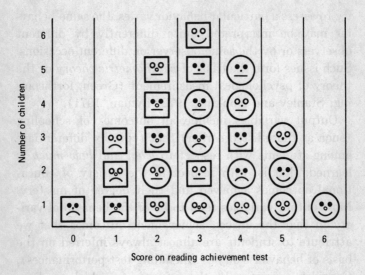

Figure 2.1

Representation of interindividual differences: distribution of reading achievement scores in a classroom of 24 children

students' reading achievement scores. Figure 2.1 shows a hypothetical distribution of scores on a test administered to a classroom of 24 children.*

Since each face in Figure 2.1 represents a particular child, you can see that the reading achievement scores in this classroom are distributed between (i.e., they range from) a low value of 0 to a high of 6. Similarly, it can be seen that one child has a score of 0, three children a score of 1, five children a score of 2, and so forth. Fur-

* The physical appearances of the characters displayed here were inspired by an entertaining, though technical, article by Chernoff (1973).

ther, it can be shown that the *average* or *mean* score on this test is 3 points, a score that was obtained by six children. (See the Green, forthcoming, volume in this series for a discussion of statistical summary measures.)

Most important for our purposes, however, is the fact that *not* every child has the same reading achievement score. True, there are some who do, which will generally be the case for any variable, be it height, age, or test performance. But the concept of interindividual variation is revealed in this example by the variation in children's scores from a low of 0 to a high of 6.

Intraindividual Variation

Just as there are differences among individuals with respect to behavioral variables, so, too, there are differences *within* an individual on a particular variable from one occasion to the next. How many times, for example, have you felt that a given test score did not reflect your true knowledge of a subject, leading you to conclude that you were not "yourself" or not "up to par" when you took the test? How many other times did you feel lucky or that everything "seemed to go right" for you? Obviously there are both *internal* and *external* factors that contribute to your performance on any particular test or task.

Internal factors include those that comprise a person's psychological (and, perhaps, physiological) state while performing a task. Alertness, motivation, and general anxiety are examples of internal factors. External factors include those factors unique to the task environment (e.g., the test conditions, the particular questions asked, the amount of time provided) that may themselves induce certain internal states such as task-specific anxiety or confidence.

At any rate, it should be clear that the unique combination of performance-related factors operating during one assessment will not be the same as those operating during another. For this reason a particular individual may well produce quite different performances on different occasions, even though his *real* ability has not changed from one occasion to the next. (To a psychometrician, an individual's real ability is represented by the *enduring* component of a test score, i.e., the component that is *not* influenced by situational factors such as those just mentioned.)

Two examples of intraindividual variation are illustrated in Figure 2.2 where the performance of a single child on 16 different occasions is portrayed for two different reading achievement test instruments (A and B). In each case, it may be determined that the child's average performance, which we regard as the best indicator of his real ability, is a score of 3 points on the test. He obtained this score four times on Test A and eight times on Test B. Note, however, that on Test A there were several occasions in which the child scored higher or lower than this (presumably because of various internal and external factors), and occasionally he scored much higher or lower. Variation in performance is clearly present on Test B as well. On this test, though, the child's scores above and below the average are neither as frequent nor as extreme as they were on Test A. That is, the child's scores on Test B are generally closer to the average than they are on Test A. In other words, the child's scores on Test B are less variable than they are on Test A, or there is less intraindividual variation in reading achievement scores associated with the second test instrument than with the first.

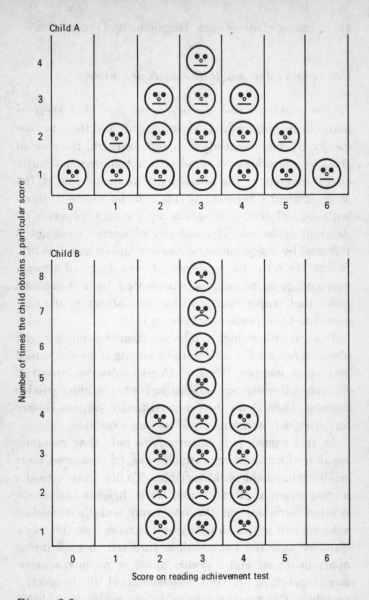

Figure 2.2
Representation of relatively large (Test A) and small (Test B) intraindividual differences: distribution of a child's reading achievement scores on 16 different occasions

Comparing Inter- and Intraindividual Variation

In the examples just discussed, we saw that there is marked intraindividual variation in addition to the commonly found variation among learners. Because of this, we must keep in mind that intraindividual variation is inherent in the assessments we make; that is, the same student's behavior is likely to be assessed differently by different observers or by the same observer on different occasions. The stability of learner variables is reflected by a psychometric concept known as *reliability*. Reliability refers to the degree of consistency of a measurement outcome and is represented by a numerical index that ranges from 0.00 (no consistency of the outcome) to 1.00 (perfect consistency).

If a variable is highly reliable, then this implies that one can repeatedly differentiate among individuals in a consistent manner. Thus, if Doris comes out ahead of Horace following one assessment of a highly reliable variable, then Doris should consistently surpass Horace on subsequent assessments of the same variable.

In this regard, it is important to note that generally speaking identification variables can be measured more reliably than behavioral variables. To illustrate, consider a comparison of Horace's and Doris' heights (an identification variable) on the one hand and their reading achievement scores (a behavioral variable) on the other. Suppose that the two children turn out to be 2 inches apart in height and 2 points apart in reading achievement according to your assessment of the respective variables. The measurement of height is influenced little, if at all, by such extraneous factors as slightly different rulers, different persons doing the measuring, and so forth. However, this is not the case with the measurement of a behavioral variable such as reading achievement. Slight variations in test content or format, as well as variations in the internal state of the student at the time of testing, can be expected to have a bearing on his or her performance. Whenever a student's performance is influenced by extraneous factors—whether they be external or internal—that cause it to vary, the variable being measured is, to some extent, unreliable.

A comparison of Figures 2.1 and 2.2 can provide an intuitive feeling for reliability. As we have just noted, when a variable is reliable, then we are able to differentiate among individuals in a consistent fashion. It turns out that a variable is reliable whenever interindividual variation is large in comparison to intraindividual variation. Thus, if we compare the performance of the child taking Test A shown in Figure 2.2 against the performance of a class of children shown in Figure 2.1, we can see that the patterns of variation are similar. In other words, the scores associated with a classroom of different students (Figure 2.1) as well as those associated with intersituational differences within the *same* student (Figure 2.2, Test A) exhibit variation across the entire range of outcomes on the reading achievement test (0–6). If every student in the classroom exhibited a pattern of intraindividual variation similar to that of the child taking Test A in Figure 2.2 (even if their real abilities were different), it would be extremely difficult to come up with a consistent ordering of students within that classroom. This is because it would be possible that the student who scored highest in the class on one occasion could score lowest on another and vice versa.

With the child taking Test B in Figure 2.2, however, the intraindividual variation is not as great. If every student in the classroom exhibited a pattern of intraindividual variation similar to that of this child, our ability to differentiate among individuals would be vastly improved. For example, with this reduced pattern of intraindividual variation, it is extremely unlikely that a student with a real score of 6 could ever be confused (in terms of reading achievement) with one with a real score of 0. The student with the real score of 6 would virtually always come out with a higher score on repeated tests. In this sense, then, Test B would be said to be more reliable than Test A.

In summary, then, the reliability of a variable amounts to a comparison of intra- and interindividual variation. The larger that interindividual variation is relative to intraindividual variation, the greater the reliability of the variable being considered. Thus, reliability reflects the extent to which we can consistently differentiate among individuals.

Inter- and Intragroup Variation

We can apply the notions of inter- and intraindividual variation and reliability to the study of *groups* of individuals as well. To illustrate, let us refer again to our classroom of 24 children in Figure 2.1. Note that each of the 24 children is depicted as a distinct individual. However, even though no two children are exactly alike, it is usually possible to identify children who are similar in some way. Frequently we can trace this similarity to one or more identification variables. For example, students are perceived as being the same age, the same sex, or from the same ethnic or socioeconomic group. Accordingly, it may be convenient (if not stereotypic—a topic to which we will return later) to group together students who have certain characteristics in common. We can then consider variation among groups, or group differences, in performance.

There are two distinct groups of children shown in Figure 2.1: the "blockheads" and the "eggheads" (referred to hereafter by the more artistically-appropriate labels of "squareheads" and "roundheads" respectively). While there is obvious variation in the achievement scores of students in Figure 2.1, it is possible that at least some of this output variation can be traced to certain input variation. In this case we can trace it to the identification variable head shape. In Figure 2.3 we have re-presented the achievement score data of Figure 2.1, according to students' head shapes. None of the information in Figure 2.1 has been changed; it has merely been rearranged to reflect what is meant by intergroup variation.

It is readily apparent from Figure 2.3 that the test performance of roundheads tends to be higher than that of squareheads (their averages are 4 and 2 points, respectively). Thus, part of the score variation in Figure 2.1 can be accounted for by the head-shape variable—roundheads tend to average two points more than squareheads on this reading test. However, it is very important to point out that despite the fact that the roundhead *average* is higher than the squarehead *average*, there is still considerable intragroup variation. Specifically, within each group there are certain students who perform as well or as poorly as certain students in the other group. In particular, this is true of any student with a score between 2 and 4, which includes 16 out of 24 or two-thirds of the total number of children in the classroom.

When individuals who belong to different groups receive the same score on a test, we say there is *overlap*

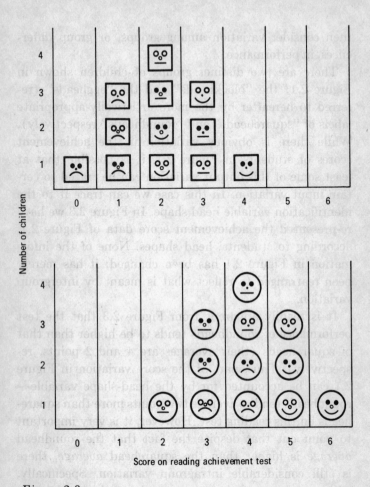

Figure 2.3
Representation of inter- and intragroup differences: distribution of reading achievement scores in a classroom

consisting of 12 squareheads (□   ) and 12 round-

heads (○   )

in the score distributions of the respective groups. The concept of overlap is crucial when considering the significance of group differences in performance, an issue that will be pursued later in the context of diagnosing learner differences (see also Jensen, 1969). And, as in the case of individuals, comparisons of inter- and intragroup variation form a basis for the reliability question which in turn speaks to the reality and importance of observed group differences.

As an example of this, note that the variability *across* groups in Figure 2.1 (i.e., ignoring the head-shape differences) is greater (0–6 points) than the variability *within* either the squarehead (0–4 points) or the roundhead (2–6 points) group in Figure 2.3. Thus, since the former (intergroup variation) is larger than the latter (intragroup variation), the head-shape variable appears to be a reliable predictor of reading achievement. On the other hand, if the inter- and intragroup variation patterns were comparable, head-shape would not be a reliable predictor of reading achievement. This further implies that the average reading achievement of roundheads and squareheads would be about the same.

Covariation and Correlation

By now you should have a good idea of what we mean by *variation*. Our development of the concept began with Figure 2.1 where we noted that if a reading achievement test were administered to a classroom of 24 children, the distribution of students' scores would reflect interindividual variation in test performance. Interestingly, the concept of interindividual variation can be extended to deal simultaneously with two or more variables—an approach that will be of use to us when considering learner differences.

Suppose, for example, that in addition to the reading achievement data from our 24 children, we also have information about how these same children performed on a spelling test. Let us assume that the range of scores on the spelling test is 0 to 7 points. Certainly we could plot a distribution of spelling scores for these children, just as we did for the reading scores in Figure 2.1. However, it is frequently more informative to deal with two variables simultaneously. This is what we have done with spelling and reading achievement in Figure 2.4. Even though the vertical axis of the graph has been redefined in this figure, a moment's study will show you that the reading test data represented here are the same as in Figure 2.1. Looking vertically within each score value on the reading test, you will find one child with a score of 0, three with a score of 1, five with a score of 2, and so forth. At the same time, this graph allows you to determine how these same children did on the spelling test. Looking horizontally within each score value on the spelling test, you will see that two children obtained a score of 0, three a score of 1, three a score of 2, and so on.

If the information contained in such a diagram is precisely the same as that contained in separate plots of the reading and spelling score distributions, then what have we gained by considering the two distributions jointly? Quite simply, since we are now able to perceive how each student did on both tests, we are able to determine whether there is any *covariation* between the two sets of scores. Covariation refers to the similarity of variation patterns in two distributions. Thus, if there is a great deal of covariation between two variables, then

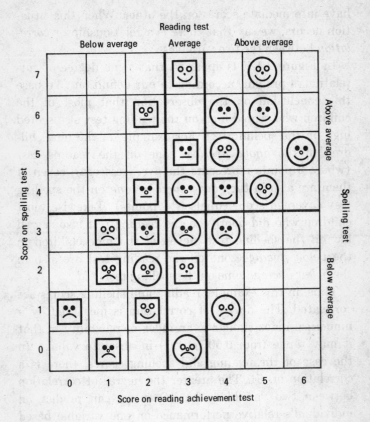

Figure 2.4
Representation of the relationship between reading achievement and spelling scores in a classroom of 24 children. (Heavy lines in this diagram are used to clarify points discussed in the text.)

those individuals with extreme scores on one variable will tend to have extreme scores on the other, and those with intermediate scores on one variable will tend to have intermediate scores on the other. When this situation occurs, we say that there is a relationship or *correlation* between the two variables.

In Figure 2.4 it is apparent that some degree of correlation is present, according to our definition. We base this conclusion on the observation that most of the children who scored high on the reading test also scored high on the spelling test. For example, of the nine children in the *above average* zone on the reading test (where 3 points represents the average score), seven of them are also in the *above average zone* on the spelling test (average score equals 3½ points). Likewise most children who did poorly on the reading test also scored low on the spelling test. Seven of the nine children in the *below average* zone on the reading test are also in the *below average* zone on the spelling test.

Thus, in this example, reading and spelling scores are correlated. The degree of correlation is measured by a numerical index similar to an index of reliability in that it may range from 0.00 to 1.00 in absolute value.* In the case of the reading and spelling scores, there is a correlation of .54. The greater the degree of correlation between two variables, the better we can predict an individual's relative performance on one variable based on knowledge of that individual's relative performance on another variable. *Relative performance* in this case means performance relative to all other individuals in the group being considered—here, performance compared to performance of all the other students in the class. When two variables are perfectly correlated (i.e., when the numerical index is 1.00 in absolute value), we

---

* This means that a correlation coefficient can take on values between −1.00 and 1.00 (for more information, see Green, forthcoming).

can predict an individual's relative performance with complete certainty. On the other hand, when two variables are uncorrelated (i.e., when the index is 0.00), we cannot predict anything about a person's relative performance on one variable from information about that person's relative performance on another.

The correlation between reading achievement and spelling in the present example (.54) suggests that we can predict an individual's relative performance with some degree of accuracy. That is, if you were asked to predict the spelling score of a child whose reading achievement score was above average, you would likely predict an above-average spelling score for that child and, what is more important, since the two variables are correlated, you could expect to be generally correct in your prediction. Those of you who are inclined to regard a correlation of .5 as indicating a 50-50 chance (as in flipping a coin) had better revise your thinking. In the present example, were you to flip a coin to predict whether a given individual was above or below average on the spelling test, your predictions would be correct about half of the time (50 percent). On the other hand, if you used the information contained in the reading achievement scores to make your spelling test predictions, you would correctly predict 14 out of the 18 distinguishable cases—7 out of the 9 students above the reading test average *plus* 7 out of the 9 students below the reading test average (see Figure 2.4). In other words, you would have been correct in almost 80 percent of your predictions.

Although it is possible to determine the correlation between any two variables of interest, we will generally be concerned here with correlating input and output variables in school-learning contexts. For, as we shall see in the following section, the remainder of the book proceeds on the assumption that a major concern of teachers and prospective teachers is *maximizing* school-learning outputs. Toward this end, we are frequently obliged to identify prospective input variables (in this book, learner characteristics) that are highly correlated with these outputs (see Chapter 3). And, further, knowing something about relationships between particular learner characteristics and school-learning outputs enables us to make rational decisions concerning the kinds of instructional programs that are suited to individual students (see Chapter 4).

Finally, it has been my experience that the notion of correlation (or, for that matter, any statistical concept that is derived from collections of individuals) tends to be put down by teachers who are rightly concerned with making decisions about "Johnny Jones," i.e., about a particular student in a particular classroom at a particular point in time. To those of you who share this concern, I offer the following. A correlation implies nothing more than that there exists a relationship between two variables, that there is a *tendency* for individuals with similar characteristics in one domain to possess similar characteristics in another domain. Certainly it is useful to know that children from rich families tend to be different from children from poor families, that those from large families *tend* to be different from those from small families, and that those from the country *tend* to be different from those from the city. Knowing that Johnny Jones is from a rich family or that he is the youngest of five children in his family or that he was raised on a farm may provide us with few or no clues about him as an individual. But, at the same time, having access to such information may help us in prescribing certain methods of instruction and curricular materials that in the past have appeared to work for students with backgrounds *similar* to Johnny's. We will repeat this theme in various forms and examples throughout this book.

A Schematic Overview

Now that you know something about the basic terms and concepts on which our discussion will rely, we can present an overview of the plan to be followed in this book. Figure 2.5 presents a schematic diagram of this plan. Adopting the position that our primary objective is one of understanding and dealing with the input variables that underlie learner differences in output, we will divide the content that remains into two major portions or stages, one called *diagnostic* and the other *prescriptive*.

Our approach involves observing learner output variation in one or more variables of interest. Let us, for the sake of continuity, say that the variable is reading achievement. Thus, having noted the learner differences, we might ask, "Can we identify any learner input variables that could help us to understand why certain children read better than others?" The process of identifying possible input variables comprises the diagnostic stage.

As we mentioned earlier, input variables include those variables that differentiate among learners in terms of the traits, abilities, and prerequisites that are related to successful output-task performance. In the context of our reading achievement example, we may posit that vocabulary knowledge is an important prerequisite to reading fluently with comprehension. If this is the case, we would expect those children with poor vocabularies

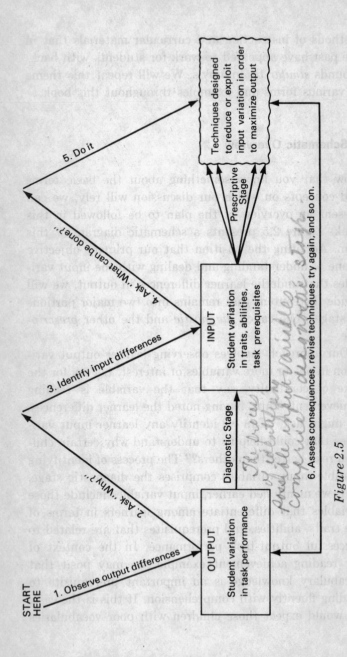

Figure 2.5
Proposed scheme for the study of learner differences

START HERE

1. Observe output differences

OUTPUT
Student variation in task performance

2. Ask "Why?"

Diagnostic Stage

The process of identifying possible input variables comprise descriptive step

INPUT
Student variation in traits, abilities, task prerequisites

3. Identify input differences

4. Ask "What can be done?"

6. Assess consequences, revise techniques, try again, and so on.

Prescriptive Stage

Techniques designed to reduce or exploit input variation in order to maximize output

5. Do it

to be poor readers—something that could be validated by comparing the reading achievement scores of students with good and poor vocabularies (as determined by a vocabulary test). The concept of validation is essential to the diagnostic stage and, consequently, will be elaborated on in Chapter 3.

While the diagnostic stage involves looking for and understanding relationships between input and output variables, our purpose in the prescriptive stage is to use this information to answer the question, "Can we *do* anything about improving students' reading?" In other words, can we devise methods or materials that capitalize on existing input variation to maximize output? We use the word maximize here in the sense of fostering achievement of the highest possible quality, both within a particular student and for as many students possible. It is in this stage where what might be called "different-strokes-for-different-folks" techniques are recommended. Through repeated evaluation and improvement of our efforts, we hope eventually to prescribe different programs of instruction for students with different input profiles to maximize output. In Chapter 4, we will look at some popular prescriptive techniques along with some examples of these techniques in action.

Chapter 5 serves as a recapitulation of the book's basic theme. In that chapter we will consider each step of the model in Figure 2.5 in terms of a concrete illustration. By doing this, I hope to convince you of the model's general utility.

Now then, is everyone ready to proceed? Some of you undoubtedly are, others not—learner differences in the rate of acquisition of new material would surely allow for this. So for those of you who are still a trifle unsure of your footing, in particular with respect to such concepts as variables, variation, reliability, and correlation, it would not be a bad idea for you to reread the relevant material in this chapter before continuing, so that everyone will enter into the following chapters with more or less a common armament of basic concepts. The technique of encouraging students to proceed at their own rates is a form of prescription to which we will return later.

Suggested Readings

Green, D. R. *Evaluating instruction.* New York: Holt, Rinehart and Winston, forthcoming.

Lyman, H. B. *Test scores and what they mean.* Englewood Cliffs, N.J.: Prentice-Hall, 1971.

Chapter 3 The Diagnostic Stage

In Chapter 2 I implied that all of the basic concepts and terms necessary for the material which follows had been introduced. I lied. We will need to add a few more as we go. For instance, it was indicated previously that the concept of validation is crucial when considering relationships between input and output variables. Let us, therefore, see what this concept means and why it is so important.

Input Variables: Valid Predictors of Output

Our chief task in the diagnostic stage of the working model proposed in Figure 2.5 is to identify accurately the variables that will provide us with leads as to why learners differ in output. Obviously in a classroom-learning context, output refers to the learned outcomes of schooling or scholastic achievement, while input refers to the multitude of characteristics that students bring with them into the learning environment.

Another way of stating the goal of the diagnostic stage is in terms of correlation. The extent to which a particular input variable is correlated with output determines whether it is a *valid* predictor of output. Thus, *validity* as it is used here may be regarded as the correlation between specified predictors (input variables) and specified criteria (output variables). We can use the numerical index of correlation to tell us how valid a particular input variable is as a predictor of some desired output, with larger correlations representing more valid predictors.

At this juncture it is important to contrast two concepts. We have referred to *reliability* as the degree of consistency of a measurement or the extent to which we can rank-order individuals similarly on different occasions in terms of a particular variable. In the latter sense, reliability may be thought of as the correlation between a given variable on one occasion *with itself* on another. On the other hand, *validity* should be thought of as the correlation between a given variable and a *different* variable.

What are the implications of this, and why do users of these concepts often confuse them? Before we can talk about one variable predicting another (validity), we must know something about the respective consistencies (reliabilities) of the constituent variables. If either the predic*ting* or the predic*ted* variable is unreliable, this will be reflected in a reduced validity for prediction. In other words, if we cannot consistently rank-order individuals with respect to the *same* variable, it is unreasonable to suppose that we can utilize such a variable to rank-order individuals with respect to a *different* variable. For example, if our reading achievement test is unreliable in the sense that there is no correspondence between who the best and who the worst readers are from one day to the next, we cannot expect such a test to give us any valid information about who the best and worst spellers are.

In such situations, you must get your own house in order (i.e., improve the reliability of the reading test— something that can be accomplished through the systematic application of psychometric principles) *before* looking into your neighbor's (i.e., before being concerned with the validity of reading test performance as a predictor of spelling performance). Extending this analogy, it is also worth remembering that even though *your* house may be in order, this does not imply that your neighbor's house is also (i.e., the reading achievement test may be perfectly reliable, but this does not necessarily imply that it will be useful in predicting spelling performance). To have valid prediction, the constituent variables *must* be reliable; yet reliable variables *might not be* valid predictors of anything.

By now you should realize that where there is variation there are learner differences. Thus, different learners wear different clothes, have different hair lengths, musical tastes, and ice cream preferences. Our concern here, however, is not with learner input variables *per se* but rather with learner input variables that are known —or presumed—to differentiate among specified learning outputs; that is, input variables that are valid predictors of these outputs. For example, even though it may be true that certain students prefer black raspberry ice cream and others prefer vanilla, it is unlikely that such information will be predictive of students' scholastic achievement. Stated differently, we have no reason to believe that the variables ice cream preference and scholastic achievement are correlated—the necessary condition for inclusion here.

On the other hand, any learner input variables that are likely to be related either to the *quality* (read kind) or *quantity* (read degree) of learning outputs could be substituted into the discussion that follows. As indicated in Chapter 1, I have elected not to provide a comprehensive summary of all potentially relevant input variables. Instead I shall simply illustrate the diagnostic stage of our working model in Figure 2.5 by means of related aspects of the most significant (at least in educational and psychological circles) of all learner input variables—*intelligence*. Following this discussion, we will look at other learner input variables that have interested educators over the years.*

Intelligence as an Input Variable

Differences in learning outputs are frequently traced to differences in intellectual ability or intelligence. But

---

* It is well known that about the best predictor of a child's performance in a given subject area (fifth grade arithmetic, for example) is his or her performance in the same subject area the

what does the word "intelligence" mean? Well, we could go on for pages or for years (as others before us have done) describing how it could be defined and measured —remember our earlier discussion of the quandaries that psychological constructs such as this create? However, it is beyond the scope of this book to do so. Instead we shall approach the problem by considering two prime input variables (one of the identification variety and the other behavioral) that in the past have been said to reflect learner differences in intelligence. These variables are *chronological age* (or, more appropriately, years of experience) and *IQ* as determined by common tests of intelligence.

When discussing age differences, we will assume that we are dealing with learners of the same IQ; and when discussing IQ differences, we will assume that the learners being compared are of the same age. Thus, although it is possible to identify five-year-old "geniuses" and eighteen-year-old "morons" on the basis of their IQ test performances, for purposes of convenience such cases will not be considered here (although we will return to this point later in the chapter). For now we might compare five-year-old and eighteen-year-old "normals" in our discussion of age as a learner input variable, and twelve-year-old "geniuses" and "morons" in our discussion of IQ. And, of course, in making such comparisons we will also assume that these learners are comparable with respect to all other input variables, such as sex, family background, and the like—otherwise we would wind up comparing apples with oranges.

---

preceding year (fourth grade arithmetic). However, previous achievement will not be singled out as an input variable for consideration here, inasmuch as it can be easily intertwined with the other input variables discussed.

*Age as Intelligence**

Chronological age, as discussed here, will include factors related to the learner's perceptual and intellectual readiness for learning. By *perceptual* I am referring to the learner's *sensory* apparatus (i.e., the senses of vision, hearing, touch, taste, and smell), which enable the learner to *perceive* the stimuli in his environment. By *intellectual* I am referring to the learner's *mental* apparatus (i.e., the brain), which enables the learner to deal with these external stimuli once they are perceived.

Just as the infant possesses visible structural characteristics that distinguish him from the adult (such as size, weight, and mobility), he also is differently equipped perceptually and intellectually for coping with and structuring his environment. Noticeably absent in the infant, for example, is the use of language as either an external (communication) or internal (thought) process. The development of perceptual and intellectual capabilities from infancy into adulthood has been carefully charted by a number of scientists from various disciplines. Among the most eminent of these researchers are Eleanor and James Gibson, Jerome Bruner, Jean Piaget of Switzerland, and L. S. Vygotsky of the Soviet Union (Ammon, 1974; Dale, 1972; Reese and Lipsitt, 1970).

Let us focus here on the investigations of Piaget and

---

* Technically it is the learner's *developmental level* (as indexed by various measures of intellectual development), rather than chronological age, that is the crucial variable in the ensuing discussion. However, the two variables are highly correlated, and since chronological age is the more familiar of the two (and conveniently measured, in terms of years or months), it will be used here as a reasonable substitute for the "real thing."

Bruner. These two individuals and their collaborators have found that intellectual development consists of *qualitatively different* stages through which the child passes as he gets older. These stages are characterized by both how the child thinks and what he can do. (Highly readable accounts of Piaget's theory, as well as its implications for education, are available—Ginsburg and Opper, 1969; Furth, 1970—as is an extensive report of the research by Bruner and his associates—Bruner, Olver, and Greenfield, 1966).

One area of common concern is the nature of the child's thought or *internal representation*. Until about age six or seven a child's thought processes seem to be governed primarily by his concrete experiences with the environment. After this age the child is not tied so completely to his environment and can execute rather simple imagistic or linguistic operations. Through these he can translate his experiences into more remote representations. However, it is generally not until about age twelve or thirteen that the child begins to exhibit a capacity to deal with abstractions such as those required for logical and analogical reasoning—a form of representation presumed to be well developed and functioning in intellectually mature adults.

Consider the following research example. Bruner and his associates have found that until six or seven years of age, the child's "view" of the world includes only that which can be seen or, more generally, that which can be experienced directly through his senses. Thus, the perceptible (external) properties of animate and inanimate objects, such as their colors, shapes, sizes, and textures, dominate his thinking about them. For instance, when shown a red ball, an apple, and a banana, and asked to put together the two that are alike; a young child is likely to group together the ball and the apple on the basis of their similar color (redness), shape (roundness), size, or some combination of these. In contrast, children older than age six or seven (and, for that matter, adults), while certainly capable of using perceptible similarities as a basis for classification, typically do not. Rather, their basis for classification resides in the categorical or functional similarities of the objects involved. Thus the apple and banana would be grouped together based on their shared category label (fruit) and/or based on their shared functional property (edible). It can be seen that these latter classification systems, which form the basis of the conceptual thought and behavior of intellectually mature individuals, tend to be more abstract in nature than are those that meet the eye of the young child.

To provide another illustration of the difference age makes in the nature of thinking, I will relate an anecdote passed on to me by a colleague, Dr. Steven Yussen. In conducting a 20-questions-type game with young children (first-graders), he noted that while these children exhibited some vague awareness that the thought processes of younger and older individuals are different, that is about as far as they could go. Consider the following dialogue between a six-year-old subject (S) and the experimenter (E), paying particular attention to the tautological responses offered by the child.

E: How would a little kid play the game differently from you?

S: Little kids are dumb! They would ask silly questions.

E: Can you give me an example of a silly question a little kid would ask?

S: Okay. (Pause). Is it something my Mommy has?
E: Why is that a silly question?
S: Because it's dumb.
E: How would a big person—an adult—play the game differently from you?
S: Big people know a lot. They would ask good questions and figure it out real fast.
E: Can you give me an example of a question that a big person would ask?
S: No!

By providing this example, I do not mean to imply that all children this age reason in such a fashion (one of the children was reported to have asked whether the object was an amphibian!), but it does not take a trained observer to recognize marked differences between the thought processes of young children and those of adults.

How do theories of intellectual development and the empirical research supporting them bear on the topic of chronological age as a predictor of learning outputs? Borrowing from an effective example provided by Paul Ammon (1974), suppose that you wished to instruct five-year-old children in the meaning of *parallel* by furnishing them with the abstract verbal definition, "Two straight lines are parallel if they are on the same plane and would never meet even if extended in length to infinity." Imagine the plight of the poor five-year-old! According to Ammon:

Because this concept of infinity requires hypothetical thinking, it seems unlikely that it could mean much more than "very long" to [children of this age], even if explained to them in great detail. In addition . . . children generally do not have the notion of a projective straight line at this stage of development. On the other hand, the learners probably would have had many concrete experiences corresponding to the words *line* (including the kind one stands in at a supermarket) and *plane* (especially the kind that flies).

Given all these conditions, it would not be surprising to find that some learners come away from the lesson with the idea that parallel refers to a long line of people waiting to board an airplane! Although it is not clear that this idea would necessarily interfere with the later learning of parallel, it is unlikely that it would be much help [p. 247].

This example highlights the importance of considering the intellectual readiness of the learner whenever something is to be taught. Whereas the linguistically and experientially advanced adolescent would likely learn something from the verbal definition of *parallel*, the five-year-old is likely to process it as jabberwocky. However, this should not imply that the five-year-old is incapable of learning anything about the parallelism concept. (We shall return to this in Chapter 4 when dealing with the prescriptive stage of our Figure 2.5 model.)

With regard to the present theme, then, clearly learners of different ages can be expected to produce qualitatively different learning outputs as a result of their qualitatively different modes of thinking. That is, there is abundant evidence to support the claim that the thought of young children is more closely tied to the concrete, to tangible instances of concepts, to the here and now; while the thought of older children has at least the potential to grasp abstractions, to formulate logical propositions (such as "if-then" relationships) and to evaluate multiple hypotheses simultaneously. Based on evidence concerning the qualitatively different *inputs* of different-aged learners, it is understandable that their *outputs* should be qualitatively different as well.

Chronological age, as an input variable, can also be invoked to account for how much we can expect a given learner to learn; that is, the amount of information that can reasonably be acquired per unit of instruction (say, one year's worth, one week's worth, or even following a single lesson) by children of different ages. Psychologists concerned with the development of intellectual abilities have provided ample evidence that from early childhood through adolescence there is a marked increase in the amount of information that can be stored in and retrieved from memory.

Along with the well-documented growth and development of the structural basis of intellect (i.e., the brain), the child's encounters with his environment are crucial in fostering the development of perceptual and linguistic skills. Included in this environmental repertoire are capabilities that have been found to emerge with age (Kreutzer, Leonard, and Flavell, 1975). Among these developing capabilities: (1) the child becomes more aware of what it means to learn something purposively (i.e., with intention) and begins to attend to a learning task in an increasingly appropriate manner, (2) the child becomes more aware of his own capacity for remembering (i.e., the amount of information that he can reasonably hope to retain in one sitting), and (3) the child begins to exhibit strategic behavior (e.g., appropriate rehearsal activity) when trying to remember something.

The research documenting the systematic intellectual changes that a child undergoes as he develops has led some researchers to propose a closer examination of our present educational policies and school curricula with an eye toward what should be taught when. For example, assuming the existence of qualitatively different stages of development, can we reasonably expect to teach a relatively complex and arbitrary system like reading to children as young as five or six years of age (Furth, 1970; Rohwer, 1972)? Interestingly, this recent inquiry is a complete turnabout from the *acceleration* approach, which is based on the philosophy that children should be taught as *much* as we can teach them as *quickly* as we can and as *soon* as we can. Furth and Rohwer have re-examined this position in light of the impressive body of research that substantiates the stages of development notions outlined here. Having done so, they contend that though it is certainly possible to make inroads into the teaching of a skill like reading even to very young children (Kohlberg, 1968)—witness the phenomenal successes of *Sesame Street* and *The Electric Company*—for a good many children trying to learn to read in the early grades is a waste of time in terms of time spent on something difficult (and even painful). For some children this time might be better spent in developing certain prerequisite skills and in exploiting their intellectual curiosity and interests. Furth and Rohwer conclude that the current practice of teaching reading in the early grades, which results in failure for many children, may contribute to a "turn off" of the child's interest in later school learning. On the other hand, if we could "decelerate" this skill to the point where reading would not be taught until the child was more intellectually prepared for it (say at about the fifth or sixth grade, age 11 or 12—although this will vary from child to child as a function of individual differences in the rate of intellectual development), then we could hope to derive two benefits.

First, we might see in the child an increased interest in school learning as a result of exposure to more curiosity-arousing and stimulating experiences during the first four or five years of school, and second, we might find that the child has an easier time learning how to read once instruction begins, as a result of his or her higher level of intellectual development, along with better-developed prerequisites (e.g., attentional, learning, and memory skills) that have been fostered in the meantime. (The interested reader should refer to Furth, 1970, and Rohwer, 1972, for other details of the argument.)

Until now we have been discussing intraindividual (or, in biological terms, *ontogenetic*) development. In other words, we have viewed development as changes in the same child as he matures. However, another kind of development stems from the intergenerational changes in a species (biologically, *phylogenetic* changes). Five-year-olds today are, on the average, intellectually more mature than five-year-olds were 20 years ago. Undoubtedly some of this may be explained in terms of Darwin's notions about the survival of the fittest. But identifiable intervening agents can also be singled out. For instance, the increasing cognizance on the part of parents and others (e.g., the media) concerning the importance of literacy in our society has resulted in conscious attempts to encourage the development of verbal skills as early as possible. Indeed, in a recent unpublished study conducted in a midwestern community, it was found that the average reading readiness scores of preschoolers increased between 1968 and 1973.* The findings of this study can be seen in Figure 3.1. If each dot represents

* I am grateful to Dr. Sylvia Rimm for making her data available to me.

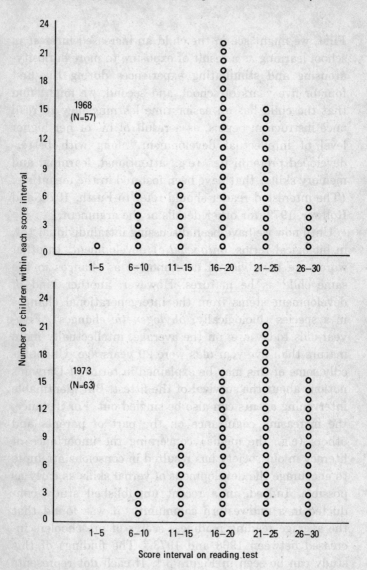

Figure 3.1

Comparison of reading readiness scores for preschoolers
in 1968 and 1973

an individual preschooler, it is easy to see the marked trend upward in reading readiness scores from one time period to the next. For example, in 1968, only 35 percent of the children tested (20 out of 57) obtained scores of 21 or better on the 30-item test. In contrast, in 1973 this figure had increased to 57 percent (36 out of 63). It is interesting to note that this particular time frame (1968 versus 1973) provided for a comparison of children from the pre- and post-*Sesame Street* eras. Certainly the noticeable increase in high readiness scores over a five-year time span is impressive. If it could be shown that the 1973 children were similar to the 1968 children with respect to other important variables—and if they indeed were found to be ardent *Sesame Street* viewers—then the increase in their scores might very well be testimony to the impact of the television program. (For a study purporting to trace other learning gains to the influence of *Sesame Street*, see Reese, 1974.) Over longer periods of time with similarly effective intervening educational agents, even more impressive increases might be anticipated (Baltes and Schaie, 1974).

Television, as an intervening agent, has also been singled out as a producer of intergenerational differences in the social behavior of young children. Increasing incidences of aggression have been attributed to television violence in recent years. The shift in children's play activity from being more gregarious in the 1930s to less so in the 1970s has also been attributed, in part, to television watching (Gaite, 1974).

To summarize, we have seen that a learner's age (or more precisely, his developmental level) provides us with valuable clues concerning what we can expect the child to learn in school. From the present standpoint, then, we may regard this identification input variable as being a valid predictor of school-learning outputs. Generally speaking, the older the learner—at least within the infancy-through-adolescence range—the more he will learn per unit of time. Similarly, knowledge of a learner's age can guide a teacher regarding the appropriate nature and level of instruction. Younger learners generally require concrete illustrations that can easily be related to their own activities and experiences. Clearly, older learners may also benefit from concrete examples —reflect on your own experiences in an obscure statistics class, or even in progressing through this book so far— although they are also likely to comprehend certain abstractions or to engage in propositional thinking and hypothetical problem solving. At the same time, as we suggested in our discussion of intergenerational changes, there is no guarantee that the statements that apply to the typical five-year-old of today will apply to the typical five-year-old of tomorrow!

IQ as Intelligence

Although chronological age provides a generally satisfactory way to deal with learner differences in intellectual development, any discussion of intelligence would be less than complete without considering the much used and abused concept of intelligence quotient or IQ. (Hunt, 1961, Tyler, 1969). At this point we must make a distinction between age and IQ as indicators of intelligence. While a stages-of-development orientation sees intelligence as a continually unfolding process, which increases with increases in age, intelligence in terms of IQ is viewed as a relative concept that remains constant from one age to the next. Both a five-year-old and a sixteen-year-old can obtain IQ scores of 100, even though the two may be stages apart in terms of the development of their modes of thinking. In IQ terminology, this difference would be shown in their different *mental ages*. Thus an individual's IQ represents an ability, not in an absolute sense, but rather with reference to other individuals of the same chronological age.

Given this distinction, there is ample support, as there is with age differences, for the claim that individuals with different IQs learn qualitatively and quantitatively different things. It might be argued that the thought of chronologically advanced but low IQ individuals (especially those classified as dull or retarded) resembles that of the young child, in the sense that it is dominated by the concrete and tangible. To use the previous example of the young child asked to group similar objects, the mentally retarded adolescent might also select an apple and a ball, rather than an apple and a banana, on the basis of their shared perceptible characteristics, rather than on the basis of their shared categorical or functional characteristics. From a quantitative point of view, retardates have been found to learn less information per unit of time in comparison to normals of the same age, again paralleling the learning of younger children of normal IQ (see Brown, 1974). Thus, like the behavior of the adolescent in comparison to that of the young child, the behavior of the high IQ student in comparison to that of the low IQ student tends to be more conceptual and strategic. Since IQ tests generally demand the use of verbal and symbolic skills, these also may be assumed to be better developed in high IQ students. Moreover, the empirical finding that IQ is to some extent predictive of scholastic achievement suggests that high IQ students tend to learn and remember more of what they are taught in school.

Despite these general tendencies, however, there are some notable exceptions that we should acknowledge. One, well documented in the psychological literature, relates to the so-called "idiot savants." Such individuals, while possessing IQs that would entitle them to retardate classifications, can retrieve unbelievable amounts of (frequently trivial) information. That is, they exhibit memory capacities that far surpass those of common folks like us. Evidence of this sort lends support to the proposition that one's IQ may or may not be indicative of his memory capacity, even though the two variables tend to be correlated in our society.

When considering age as an input variable, we implied that learners of different ages could be expected to differ in their intellectual outputs as a result of variations in the nature and number of previous encounters with their environments. Similarly, differences in IQ among individuals of the same age have been thought to result from differences in the learners' environmental histories. Thus, even though two students may be exactly the same chronological age, they may not be the same *experiential* age. That is, they may not have been exposed to exactly the same sources of environmental stimulation during early childhood and later development. (Contrast, as an obvious example, the experiential background of a student from a wealthy professional family with that of a student whose family is on welfare.) However, even with the potential influence of *environmental* factors on an individual's resultant intelligence, we cannot ignore the vast amount of evidence that implicates *hereditary* (genetic) factors. Indeed, for some, hereditary factors are believed to comprise the major contributors to an individual's intelligence (or at least to his or her IQ). The age old nature-nurture or heredity-environment controversy, which debates the respective contributions of each to IQ, has been rekindled in recent years and has snowballed to include identification variables such as sex, social class, and ethnic group membership (*Psychology Today*, 1973). The current furor over this question is bound to have social and political repercussions for years to come.

Let us attempt to summarize this section with explicit reference to the two psychometric concepts introduced earlier, namely, reliability and validity. With respect to reliability, we must conclude that whatever it is that IQ tests measure, it is measured reliably. It is not uncommon to find IQ tests that possess reliability indices in the .90s, suggesting that such tests are very good at consistently differentiating between high and low scorers. In other words, with reliabilities of this magnitude it is extremely unlikely that two individuals who obtain respective IQ scores of 120 and 80 on one occasion would ever reverse positions on subsequent IQ assessments. Given so high a reliability, we surely can determine who the "best" and "worst" are on whatever underlying trait or ability it is that an IQ test taps.

But exactly what are we tapping? This brings us to a discussion of our second psychometric friend, validity. Opponents of IQ testing have argued that whatever we are measuring, even if it is measured reliably, is measured with little or no validity—remember peeking into your neighbor's house? At this time there is no consensus on the kinds of traits and abilities being tapped by IQ tests. Do such tests reflect more or less innate intelligence, the ability to use facts and skills that were previously learned, or just a general adeptness at coping with tests like this?

On the other hand, for certain proponents of IQ testing, the question of the validity of the psychological construct being tapped is secondary. What is of primary importance is the validity of the test as a predictor of societal criteria that are deemed important (occupational level and income, for example). With respect to criteria relevant to our focus in this book, IQ is a useful predictor of school-learning outputs, frequently correlating in the .50s or more with school achievement measures (cf. Figure 2.4 for a schematic representation of a correlation of this magnitude). The usefulness of certain IQ tests is especially noticeable when it comes to identifying children with severe learning disabilities. This is not surprising since the types of items that make up the commonly used IQ tests are fashioned after Alfred Binet's original item assortment that was developed to identify learning-disabled children. Thus, since IQ is a valid predictor of various learning outputs, we can consider it a relevant learner input variable.

At the same time, we should remember what a correlation does and does not imply. It does not imply, for example, that an individual with a high IQ will necessarily be a good learner, or that one with a low IQ will of necessity be a poor learner. Moreover, within certain ethnic and racial minorities of our society, IQ scores cannot always be regarded as valid indices of learning potential. Since the actual content of these tests may be unfamiliar to students with experiential backgrounds different from the backgrounds of those who served as standards (or norms) for the test, we cannot determine whether a low IQ score represents low learning potential or just a general lack of familiarity with the item content. Indeed, it has been argued that the correlation between IQ and learning is quite low for some minorities (Jensen, 1969).

Additional Input Variables

Intellectual Styles and Strategies

Closely related to the topic of what a learner can do intellectually, is the question of how he does it. Loosely speaking, we may think of the former as an intellectual *product* and the latter as an intellectual *process*, albeit this distinction is not completely satisfactory. Thus, even though two learners may be at the same intellectual level in terms of age and IQ, there is evidence to suggest that they may exhibit quite different styles and strategies in learning and problem solving.

Bissell, White, and Zivin (1971) have examined differences in learners' preferred *sensory modalities* for acquiring new knowledge. For example, certain children may learn a science lesson about the Krebs cycle best by reading a description of it in a textbook (*visual* processing of verbal material.) Others may learn more from listening to the same description on a record or tape (*auditory* processing). Still others may not learn optimally until the cycle is made more concrete for them through the use of illustrations, movies, or demonstrations (*visual-pictorial* processing) or through actual experimentation (*kinesthetic* or *tactual* processing). Of course, various combinations of the above are possible and frequently desirable, not to mention other forms of learning such as one-to-one tutorial sessions and small group discussions in which the student's own *vocal* apparatus is engaged. The important thing to remember here is that different children come to prefer different modes of sensory input and, as we shall see later, if we are aware of these differences, we should be able to use that information in the prescriptive stage of our working model.

Conveniently, modality preferences may be related back to the age-stage concepts discussed previously. Bruner and his colleagues (1966) have characterized stages of development in terms of essentially three different modes of representing incoming information. Specifically, there is a general developmental progression from a propensity in the young child to represent information kinesthetically or in an *enactive* mode to a propensity in the elementary-school-aged child to represent it through the formation of visual images in an *ikonic* mode to a propensity in the adolescent to represent it through language and symbols in a *symbolic* mode. (Note how closely this sequence corresponds to the developing child's increasing ability to abstract and to reason logically. This also incorporates the previously discussed perceptible-to-categorical shift in classificatory systems.) For example, the young child learning the basic arithmetic operations by building 4 rows of 5 sticks and counting the resulting 20 sticks is learning enactively. The older child who learns through textbook illustrations that if one apple costs 5 cents, then 4 apples cost 20 cents, is learning ikonically. The adolescent learning that if $x = .8y$ and $xy = 20$, then $x = 4$, $y = 5$, is learning symbolically. (Given recent developments in the teaching of mathematical concepts, the "New Math" for example, aspects of the preceding example may have to be modified somewhat.)

In addition to different modalities for learning, different intellectual styles have also been identified and studied in learners (Kogan, 1971). Such styles include the learner's characteristic *tempo* in question answering and problem solving (Does he answer impulsively and often erroneously, or does he reflect upon his answer before offering it?); his characteristic attention to *details* as opposed to the more general properties of objects (Does he visually pick things apart, or does he put them together?); the nature and breadth of his characteristic *classification* systems (What kinds of things does he tend to view as similar, à la Bruner's perceptible-categorical distinction just reviewed, and how tolerant is he to include—or reluctant to exclude—various category instances?).

There are currently available a number of perceptual tasks that can be used to diagnose an individual's intellectual style. For example, a task that requires matching a target figure with various alternatives yields time and accuracy scores. In combination these scores identify "impulsive" and "reflective" individuals—impulsives being those individuals who respond faster and make more errors in comparison to their peers (Kogan, 1971). In Chapter 4 we will see how information of this type might be of use to us in prescribing instructional treatments.

An additional and highly interesting intellectual style that differentiates learners has been reported by Pask and Scott (1972). Some learners ("serialists") tend to "learn, remember and recapitulate a body of information in terms of string-like [mental] structures where items are related by simple data links: formally, by 'low order relations'"; whereas others ("holists") tend to "learn, remember and recapitulate as a whole: formally, in terms of 'high order relations' [p. 218]." This is an intriguing finding to which we will return in Chapter 4.

As we shall see, the essence of learning modality and learning style constructs is frequently not one of how much is learned but rather one of how information is represented and organized (mentally) by the learner. Hypothesizing about different forms of internal representation and then obtaining evidence to corroborate such hypotheses presents a formidable task for the cognitive psychologist. However, this is a sorely needed process in our working model's prescriptive stage insofar as the selection of appropriate instructional methods, materials, and criterion measures is concerned.

Finally, as was true in the case of intellectual ability, it has been hypothesized that certain modality and style patterns emerge from the learner's previous child rearing and socialization experiences. Genetic arguments, however, are not as common here. Moreover, various styles, in particular, have been related to various personality traits. For example, tolerance for ambiguity or uncertainty has been related to risk-taking behavior. Certain styles have also been related to certain interpersonal behaviors such as communication and manipulative skills (Kogan, 1971).

Socioeconomic and Cultural Factors

Variables reflecting intellectual abilities and patterns have been singled out as prime candidates to be considered when predicting learning outputs. And, as we have mentioned, some researchers believe that the child's environmental experiences are crucial to determining the child's rate of intellectual development and the nature of his resultant intellectual skills, strategies, and styles. Preeminent among the environmental contributors to a student's intellectual modus operandi are those associated with the home and family.

The child's socioeconomic and cultural milieu determine, in large part, the nature and variety of experiences provided him as he develops. Obviously the child who comes from a family that gives little or no support for intellectual and linguistic activity in the home—through the provision of appropriate toys, records, books, problem-solving games, in addition to parent-child interaction and communication (apart from reprimands)—will enter school with a considerably different set of background experiences and skills in comparison to the child who comes from a family in which such activity is not merely provided but encouraged.

One can readily enumerate a host of measures that might contribute to a family background index (parents' occupations, incomes, and own level of education being among the most salient). However, such information is not always easy to come by—nor should it be, given contemporary concern for the private rights of individuals—although in some cases it should be obvious (e.g., in the case of students attending exclusive private schools on the one hand and those attending Title I schools on the other).

While there are undoubtedly *intellectual* components underlying the relationship between family background variables and school learning (Coleman, et al., 1966), nonintellectual components such as those of the *attitudinal* variety may be assumed to be involved as well.

Motivation to Learn

A significant attitudinal component is the student's motivation to learn in school. Motivation to learn is a behavioral variable that has been defined and measured in a number of different ways. We have seen that an individual's family background may influence what he learns in the home. If the family also conveys to the child a negative or indifferent attitude toward the value of education in general, this can have profound implications for the student's resultant attitude toward learning in school. Of concern to us here is the finding that student attitudes toward learning frequently serve as a useful index for predicting scholastic success.

In some cases a student's attitude or motivation to learn may be an even more valid predictor of his or her subsequent academic achievements than general intelligence or specific abilities are. For example, there are many students with average or below average IQs whose attitude in school (resulting from family influences, the student's self-concept, or whatever) is one of extreme determination and motivation to succeed, which they do —through study and hard work. Such students have been referred to as "overachievers" in the literature, since their scholastic achievement exceeds what would have been predicted on the basis of their IQ alone. The opposite case is that of the "underachiever," the student whose IQ is above average, yet he is not performing up to expectation in school. (This is often due to laziness or lack of motivation.) We will return to this example in the concluding section of this chapter.

As with most of the other input variables discussed, a number of instruments are available to diagnose students' motivation to learn (Day and Berlyne, 1971; deCharms, 1971). Similarly, attitude questionnaires may also provide helpful information concerning students' expressed attitudes (Shaw and Wright, 1967).

Other input variables thought to be related to learning outputs include the learner's sex, birth order, family size, and various traits in the intellectual domain (e.g., creativity) and the personality-social domain (e.g., extraversion and morality). (Some of these variables are discussed at length in Lesser, 1971b—see chapters by Torrance, Schmuck, and Kohlberg and Turiel in particular—as well as in the more recent work by Brophy and Good, 1974.)

Some Concluding Remarks

As we have just seen, the diagnostic stage of our working model operates in the following manner: (1) We note that there are marked differences among learners in the quantity and quality of learning outputs; (2) We ask why; (3) We hypothesize about—and ultimately identify—input variables that help us to understand these output differences. Thus we find through careful research that input variables such as intelligence, motivation, and the like are indeed valid predictors of learning outputs. In the next chapter we will see how we can use this kind of information to our (or, rather, to our learners') advantage. But before we get to the prescriptive stage, we must look briefly at a couple important issues related to the diagnostic stage.

Be Aware of What Group Differences Imply

One of the concerns related to the diagnostic stage is inter- and intragroup variability. When we discussed this issue in Chapter 2, we noted with reference to Figure 2.3 that although the variable head shape seemed to differentiate well for reading test performance, in that roundheads outscored squareheads by an average of two points, it did not do so perfectly. If it had, then every roundhead would have surpassed every squarehead in reading such that there would be no overlap in the respective reading score distributions. As can be seen from Figure 2.3, however, this was clearly not the case. A number of squareheads have reading scores that are as high or higher than certain roundheads.

The principle operating here can be traced back to the notion of correlation. Unless two variables (here the input variable of head shape and the output variable of reading achievement) are perfectly correlated (i.e., the associated numerical index is 1.00 in absolute value), then the outputs related to the different input classifications will overlap to some extent. This implies that while a particular input variable may help us to explain some of the output variation, typically it will not account for all of it. In terms of the present example, even though the head shape classification variable is useful in explaining output differences, it is not a sufficient explainer. This insufficiency may be traced to the previously noted overlap in the squarehead and roundhead reading achievement distributions or, stated a different way, to the wide variation in reading achievement scores obtained by students within each head-shape classification.

Why is there variation within classification? Virtually no output variables can be completely explained by a single input variable. As noted before, for example, even though there is a relationship between IQ and scholastic achievement, we can easily find instances of high IQ students with poor scholastic achievement ("underachievers") and vice versa ("overachievers"). This kind of evidence suggests that not just one learner input variable (e.g., IQ) but a number of learner input variables (including motivation) combine to explain various learner outputs.

In other words, even though two individuals may be comparable with respect to one input variable, they may differ considerably with respect to others, which in turn account for differences in their respective outputs. Two recommendations for teachers follow from this observation.

First, whenever possible a teacher should attempt to identify additional input variables that can be examined in conjunction with the major input variable of interest. Thus, in looking at IQ as a predictor of scholastic achievement, you might do well to consider motivation, as well as other potentially relevant variables, along with it. We can illustrate this kind of multivariable or *input-profile* approach in its simplest form (i.e., for two input variables) for the roundhead-squarehead example of Figure 2.3.

As stated earlier, even after specifying head shape as a relevant input variable, we are left with some inexplicable instances of low-achieving roundheads and high-achieving squareheads. Suppose we posit that an attitudinal factor, as reflected by smiling or frowning faces, is a crucial companion to head shape. Specifically, let us imagine that the available literature suggests that roundheads with positive attitudes (smiling faces) should be the best readers and squareheads with negative attitudes (frowning faces) should be the worst readers. Pulling apart the information in Figure 2.3 and re-presenting it in Figure 3.2, we can see clearly that when these two input variables (head shape and facial expression) are considered jointly, there is perfect prediction. All the smiling roundheads are the best readers in the class, and all the frowning squareheads are the worst. By specifying a second relevant input variable, we were able to

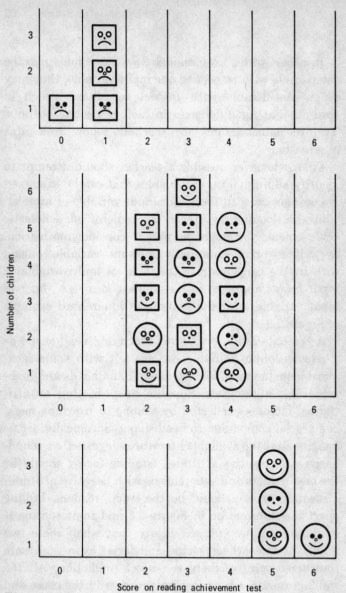

Figure 3.2
Removing the between-group overlap in Figure 2.3 by considering a second input variable

increase the roundhead-squarehead reading achievement difference noted in Figure 2.3 to the point where the overlap in scores has been eliminated.

Of course, this example is an idealized one and greatly oversimplified in comparison to the complex relationships that exist in the real world. In order to achieve maximal differentiation between groups, many more than two input variables must undoubtedly be included in the profile, and even then some degree of overlap will result from additional, unknown learner input variables. Nonetheless, the basic rationale behind the approach is reasonable and should be understood by educators.

The second recommendation is that you should not lose sight of the fact that group differences reveal tendencies, not truths. It is easy to fall into a trap in which knowing that group differences exist leads you to incorrect predictions of performance associated with individuals within groups. The knowledge that roundheads *as a group* tend to perform better than squareheads *as a group* should not color your perception of Stella Squarehead *as an individual*. As we have seen, there are a number of reasons (attitude, for example) why Stella might be a much better reader than would be anticipated strictly on the basis of her membership in the squarehead group. To expect her to be a poor reader simply because she is a squarehead is not only unwarranted on the basis of known between-group overlap but also constitutes a great personal injustice to Stella as an individual (Jensen, 1969). Another reason for avoiding such stereotype situations involves the common sense notion of self-fulfilling prophecies, a subject that has received considerable notoriety in the educational research community of late (McNamee, 1971; Rosenthal, 1971).

Beware of Stereotyping Students

The recent work of Brophy and Good (1974) provides an excellent review of the research on self-fulfilling prophecies in the classroom. The central message of the research is that the relationship between student input and output variables is frequently exaggerated through teacher stereotypes and expectations derived from teachers' awareness of the input variable information. Thus, students whom teachers expect to do well in school (due to their apparent brightness, attentiveness, attractiveness, or even because their older sibling did well the year before) will do well in part as a result of this expectation, and students whom teachers expect to do poorly (due to their similarly perceived negative qualities) will do poorly in part for the same reason.

Obviously the argument has profound implications, and the basic premise is intuitively convincing, notwithstanding the fact that the empirical research on which the premise received its initial publicity (Rosenthal and Jacobson, 1968) was not particularly sound (see Elashoff and Snow, 1971). Consider, for example, this description by Brophy and Good (1974) of the possible sequence of events that could occur as a result of inappropriate stereotypes.

If a teacher harbors an inappropriate but rigid expectation that a particular student is not capable of doing the work assigned to his class or group, the teacher is likely to "give up" psychologically on this student, perhaps going through the motions of teaching him but not doing so with serious determination and with the expectation that the student will learn. This initial teacher expectation can set off a series of circular and mutually reinforcing events. First, the teacher is likely to treat the student with less enthusiasm than he treats other students, to call on the student less frequently, to persist in seeking responses with him less often and with less determination, and, in general, to make only half-hearted attempts to teach the student and to be relatively unconcerned when the student fails. Furthermore, since our expectations affect our perceptions as well as our behavior, the teacher will have a general tendency to notice evidence of failure in the student and at the same time will be less likely to notice the student's successes. . . . This mechanism of selective perception . . . will of course reinforce the teacher's low expectations regarding the student. . . .

While the above experiences are occurring within the teacher, experiences are occurring within the student which also reinforce the vicious circle. First, to the extent that the student is being taught less, both in terms of quantity of material taught and quality of teaching (enthusiasm, determination, patience, and support), he will learn relatively less than his classmates. The longer this continues, the further behind he will fall, thus further confirming the teacher's low expectations. In addition, the student's motivation is likely to be eroded, partly because he will be continually falling further behind and finding the work more difficult, and partly because he is likely to diagnose correctly the teacher's treatment of him and to reach the conclusion that the teacher does not think that he is very bright or very likely to be able to handle the material. This in turn is likely to lead to an attitude of frustration, apathy, and defeatism, producing symptomatic behavior such as withdrawal from the classroom and a tendency to give up easily rather than persist when difficulties in learning are encountered. To the extent that any of these effects occur in the student, the quality of his work will further deteriorate and the teachers' [sic] low expectations for him will be further reinforced [pp. 36–37].

Introspectively, we probably all can gather enough evidence of the phenomenon in operation. Of contemporary concern, for instance, are traits and behaviors associated with maleness and femaleness in our society. Are these characteristics innate and predetermined or do they result from societal attitudes and expectations? (Hopefully Billie Jean King laid one such expectation to rest in her 1973 tennis match with Bobby Riggs!)

Can you, as a teacher, recount any instances in which you gave preferential treatment (no matter whether intentional nor how small the degree) to the seemingly more bright, motivated, personable student, or in which you gave discriminatory treatment to the homely student or to the one whose handwriting was difficult to read? As you can see from the latter example, this phenomenon can manifest itself in many different contexts. Not only do our views of students' characteristics influence how we teach them (in terms of the tolerance we have for their mistakes, the pace at which we proceed, the amount of reinforcement we provide, etc.), but students' characteristics may also influence how we evaluate them (in terms of the effort we expend in trying to decipher responses, the tolerance we have for slight deviations from "correct" answers, the degree to which we "read" additional information into student responses, etc.). This is especially true when such evaluations are based on subjective data in which the role of the evaluator is substantial. Is it fair for a bright child to receive additional breaks like this, which in turn can only reinforce stereotypes by exaggerating existing differences among students or groups?

It is, in part, in response to concerns such as these that an increasing number of school districts have been eliminating IQ information from students' records on the grounds that such information can lead to more harm than good. The teacher who is aware that expectations can lead to partiality in the classroom, can try to prevent such damage from occurring in the name of fairness to all students. As Brophy and Good (1974) point out:

. . . it should be kept in mind that expectations are normal and ubiquitous and are neither good nor bad in themselves. Their potential for interfering with teaching goals is determined not by their presence or absence, since they are ubiquitously present, but instead by their general degree of accuracy and flexibility and their potential for adjustment in response to change in the behavior of the student [p. 35].

My own personal expectation is that we have belabored this issue long enough. So, having covered the diagnostic preliminaries of Figure 2.5, let us move on to the prescriptive stage of our working model.

Suggested Readings

Ammon, P. R. The cognitive approach to intellectual development. In W. D. Rohwer, Jr., P. R. Ammon, & P. Cramer (Eds.), *Understanding intellectual development*. New York: Holt, Rinehart and Winston, 1974.

Baltes, P. B., & Schaie, K. W. Aging and IQ: The

myth of the twilight years. *Psychology Today*, 1974, **7**, 35–40.

Bissell, J., White, S., & Zivin, G. Sensory modalities in children's learning. In G. S. Lesser (Ed.), *Psychology and educational practice*. Glenview, Ill.: Scott, Foresman and Co., 1971.

Brophy, J. E. & Good, T. L. *Teacher-student relationships: Causes and consequences*. New York: Holt, Rinehart and Winston, 1974.

Dale, P. S. *Language development: Structure and function*. New York: Holt, Rinehart and Winston, 1972.

Day, H. I., & Berlyne, D. E. Intrinsic motivation. In G. S. Lesser (Ed.), *Psychology and educational practice*. Glenview, Ill.: Scott, Foresman and Co., 1971.

de Charms, R. From pawns to origins: Toward self-motivation. In G. S. Lesser (Ed.), *Psychology and educational practice*. Glenview, Ill.: Scott, Foresman and Co., 1971.

Furth, H. G. *Piaget for teachers*. Englewood Cliffs, N.J.: Prentice-Hall, 1970.

Gaite, A. J. H. Preschool play behavior: Then and now. *Instructor*, 1974, **84**, 36.

Ginsburg, H. & Opper, S. *Piaget's theory of intellectual development: An introduction*. Englewood Cliffs, N.J.: Prentice-Hall, 1969.

Kogan, N. Educational implications of cognitive styles. In G. S. Lesser (Ed.), *Psychology and educational practice*, Glenview, Ill.: Scott, Foresman and Co., 1971.

Kohlberg, L. Early education: A cognitive-developmental view. *Child Development*, 1968, **39**, 1013–1062.

Kohlberg, L., & Turiel, E. Moral development and moral education. In G. S. Lesser (Ed.), *Psychology and educational practice*. Glenview, Ill.: Scott, Foresman and Co., 1971.

McNamee, G. E. Institutional stereotypes and educational practice. In G. S. Lesser (Ed.), *Psychology and educational practice*. Glenview, Ill.: Scott, Foresman and Co., 1971.

Race, intelligence and genetics. In *Psychology Today*, 1973, **7**, 79–101 (articles by A. R. Jensen, B. Rice, and T. Dobzhansky).

Rohwer, W. D., Jr. Decisive research: A means for answering fundamental questions about instruction. *Educational Researcher*, 1972, **1** (7), 5–11.

Rosenthal, R. Teacher expectations and their effects upon children. In G. S. Lesser (Ed.), *Psychology and educational practice*. Glenview, Ill.: Scott, Foresman and Co., 1971.

Schmuck, R. A. Influence of the peer group. In G. S. Lesser (Ed.), *Psychology and educational practice*. Glenview, Ill.: Scott, Foresman and Co., 1971.

Torrance, E. P. Creativity in the educational process. In G. S. Lesser (Ed.), *Psychology and educational practice*. Glenview, Ill.: Scott, Foresman and Co., 1971.

Chapter 4 The Prescriptive Stage

The Traditional Approach to Schooling

In the beginning—both historically and in grade school
—a common strategy was first to define appropriate educational objectives that all students should attain and
then to provide students in a classroom with the instruction assumed optimal for attaining those objectives.
There are three assumptions (the first two explicit, the
third implicit) underlying this strategy: (1) What is
appropriate for one student in the way of educational
objectives is appropriate for another; (2) What is optimal in the way of instruction for one student in a classroom is optimal for all students in the classroom; and
(3) Exactly what the appropriate objectives and opti-

mal means of instruction are is known by those powers who say what they are.

It is easy to see from the first two assumptions associated with this approach to schooling that no provision is made for learner differences. This is true both for the goals of schooling and the means required to attain those goals. What is right for one is assumed to be right for all. As Cronbach (1967) has noted, under this approach learner differences ". . . were taken into account chiefly by eliminating students. Less successful students (and those from poorer families) dropped out all along the way [p. 24]." Although most contemporary educators would disavow affiliation with any such "survival of the fittest" approach, variants of the theme are still manifested within particular facets of our educational institutions. For example, within almost any college or university, especially at the graduate level or in professional schools, we can identify courses and programs of study designed to weed out those students who cannot "cut it." This attitude also clearly prevails in the exclusive preparatory schools at the secondary and, more recently, even at the primary levels.

While some individuals attempt to justify this approach to schooling in the name of quality control, in the name of learner differences as discussed in this book it is indefensible. It ignores, for example, the possibility that many so-called "unfits" turned out that way because the means of instruction were, in fact, not optimal for them. Had alternative means been provided, success rather than failure might have been the result. We shall see this argument through to its logical conclusion throughout this chapter. We will also consider some alternatives to the pseudoegalitarian "one-for-all' instructional approach to schooling. In accordance with the prescriptive stage of our model, these alternatives typically will consist of the use of instructional methods and materials suited to the input characteristics of individual learners—something clearly at odds with the second assumption of the traditional approach described earlier.*

As we proceed, we shall also call into question the first assumption of the traditional approach, namely, that the goals of schooling should be the same for all students. In this context, techniques that provide for vastly different objectives for different students, as well as those that provide for different aspects of the same objective for different students, will be considered (Cronbach, 1967; Glaser, 1972). Certain of these techniques relate to the third assumption of the traditional approach inasmuch as the student's role in educational decision making (in terms of means and goals) is explicitly acknowledged.

What follows, then, is a discussion of instructional approaches designed to maximize output both for a given learner and for as many learners as possible. Specifically, in this chapter we shall present the basic rationale behind each approach and provide illustrations of each by means of empirical data, generally gathered in laboratory-type experiments and/or real-world educational applications. Let us begin by considering some of the earliest efforts in this direction.

---

* The approach we will adopt here is also compatible with Glaser's (1972) distinction between "selective" and "adaptive" modes of instruction.

Initial Approaches to Learner Differences

Teaching the Same Material at Different Levels

How long ago were you instructed in the concept of "parallel"? Maybe not as long ago as you might think. Turn back to the definition of parallel on p. 43 of the last chapter and read it, as well as the subsequent discussion related to the concept, stopping when you reach the end of the excerpt from Ammon (1974).

At this point I must admit to a wrongdoing. I did not give you Ammon's complete discussion in Chapter 3 for he goes on to state:

Had the concept been presented at an intuitive level, the result might have been much more satisfactory. The learners probably could have understood that two objects, such as two pencils, are parallel when they are placed side by side and point in the same direction. This understanding of parallel, though not complete, is on the right track and could be refined and restructured at later stages of development [p. 247].

This gets to the heart of Bruner's (1960) often quoted and misinterpreted claim that it is possible to teach concepts from any subject matter in some "intellectually honest" form to students at any stage of development. As Ammon points out, the young child going through the "pencil routine" will certainly not have the same depth of understanding of the geometric concept "parallel" as a tenth-grade geometry student, but neither will "parallel" feed into the same knowledge network for the tenth-grader as it does for his teacher or as it did for Pythagoras or Euclid. But surely some of the rudiments of the parallelism concept and, perhaps, some applications of it are accessible even to the five-year-old. Certainly to conclude that such a child is incapable of learning anything about parallelism overstates the case. As Bruner reiterates in a later work:

Since most subjects can be translated into forms that place emphasis on doing, or upon the development of appropriate imagery, or upon symbolic-verbal encoding, it is often possible to render the end result to be achieved in a simpler, more manageable form so that the child can move more easily and deeply to full mastery [Bruner, Olver, and Greenfield, 1966, p. 30].

This example illustrates what we mean when we speak of teaching aspects of the same material at different levels to learners with different input characteristics. Indeed, the vast majority of educational institutions implicitly operate under this very "spiral curriculum" philosophy (Bruner, 1960). Instruction at successively higher grade levels (generally in two- or three-grade steps) consists of a return to previously acquired concepts and knowledge bases and builds upon them by reformulating them in terms of more complete, and more technically correct, understanding. In a sense, instruction geared to capitalizing on any prerequisite skills or knowledge may be regarded as a generalization of the spiral curriculum notion (Bruner, 1960). (See the Gagné, 1974, volume in this series for a discussion of vertical and lateral transfer.)

Although we have focused our discussion of the "same thing, different levels" approach on age differences, extensions (e.g., IQ, social class, and even intergenerational differences) are easy to make. One of the most obvious of these, and one still in vogue in many educational systems, consists of grouping or tracking students within the same grade level on the basis of their current level of achievement with respect to particular subject matter. Students are homogeneously grouped (frequently, but not always, in different classrooms), and each group is provided with instruction and materials assumed to be geared to a level appropriate for students within that particular track. (Lesser, 1971a, has criticized ability grouping, partly on the basis of the possibility of undesirable consequences of teacher and student "expectancies.")

Although in theory a "same thing, different levels" philosophy allows as many students as possible to attain the same goal since each student is taught at his or her own "level," a more detailed examination reveals that in practice the result is otherwise. Clearly, even though all students are given instruction in the same nominal subject area (e.g., fifth-grade arithmetic), the lower-tracked Stella Squarehead may be struggling through her times tables while upper-tracked Roger Roundhead may be acquiring a conceptual understanding of the distributive property of the multiplication operation. It is likely that these differences will lead to *qualitatively* different educational outcomes for the two students (in this case, in arithmetic knowledge). Thus, to conclude that students in different tracks are learning the same things is as wrong as concluding that students at different ages have the same breadth of understanding of the concept "parallel." A similar argument may be made with regard to comparisons of different instructional methods for teaching the "same" material—even when learner input differences are not considered. That is, qualitatively different learned outcomes may be the result.

Teaching Different Things to Different Students

Suppose that Stella Squarehead aspires to be the lead tuba player in a symphony orchestra and that Roger Roundhead aspires to be an authority on Greek mythology. It would seem to make sense, then, to provide Stella with as much tuba-playing instruction and as many related experiences as possible and Roger with as much Homer-reading instruction and as many related experiences as possible. (This does not imply, however, that Stella and Roger should be denied educational experiences in the other's domain nor that tastes of various other educational experiences should be withheld. Cronbach's, 1967, distinction between unique and common educational goals is relevant here.)

The obvious philosophy behind the "different things, different students" approach is to provide the instruction and experiences directly related to the occupational goals of individual students. Not coincidentally, many occupational goals may be couched in terms of educational objectives. A consideration of students' intellectual abilities in conjunction with an examination of their present interests and vocational aspirations calls for prescriptions of different programs of instruction for different students. Psychologists and counselors at both the secondary and college levels have used the well-known vocational aptitude tests and interest inventories for just such prescriptions. Among schools, manifestations of this approach may be found in the various vocational school programs. Within schools, manifestations of the approach may be found in the various elective courses offered. In each case, the translation of students' differing vocational plans into differing educational objectives is apparent.

One of the more outspoken proponents of a "different goal" philosophy of schooling has been Arthur Jensen (e.g., 1969). Unfortunately, much of the force of his arguments has been lost in the stir over what some believe is Jensen's advocacy of different instructional programs for students of different racial and socioeconomic groups (Karier, 1974). But if we strip away the racial and ethnic overtones, the heart of Jensen's message is clear, as viewed from the present perspective of different educational objectives for individual students with different intellectual abilities and vocational aspirations.

If diversity of mental abilities, as of most other human characteristics, is a basic fact of nature . . . and if the ideal of universal education is to be successfully pursued, it seems a reasonable conclusion that schools and society must provide a range and diversity of educational methods, programs, and goals, and of occupational opportunities, just as wide as the range of human abilities. Accordingly, the ideal of equality of educational opportunity should not be interpreted as uniformity of facilities, instructional techniques, and educational aims for all children. Diversity rather than uniformity of approaches and aims would seem to be the key to making education rewarding for children of different patterns of ability. The reality of individual differences thus need not mean educational rewards for some children and frustration and defeat for others [Jensen, 1969, p. 117].

The previous examples of vocational schools and elective courses within schools may be regarded as instances in which students are granted some degree of control over their academic and occupational destinies. That is, students are free to some extent to choose the programs of instruction that will enable them to be what it is they want to be. According to this philosophy, the student (perhaps with the assistance of a parent or counselor) is assumed to be capable of defining the unique educational objectives that are appropriate for him.* However, even with such an individualized approach, although the stated educational goals are in the hands of the student, the means for attaining those goals remain in the hands of the teacher. Thus, once a student has defined the program of study he desires, he must then take more or less fixed courses of fixed content (Cronbach, 1967). This is not true, however, of more recent manifestations of the "different things, different students" philosophy, as we will see later in this chapter.

Dealing with Learner Input Differences

In the examples just given, we can distinguish between two basic techniques for dealing with learner differences in input. In the discussion that follows, we will adopt

---

* Nonetheless it is worthwhile to take heed of Karier's (1974) observation that "One of the great myths of the twentieth century has been the belief that a differentiated curriculum based on assumed individual abilities and needs would result in increased choice on the part of the individual. From the very beginning of the century, the differentiated curriculum has served to channel, control, and limit the choices of individuals [p. 300]."

Cronbach and Snow's (1976) *compensatory* and *capitalization* labels to make the distinction (see Figure 4.1).

The technique of teaching aspects of the same material at different levels may be regarded as a *compensation* in that students deficient in some skill or ability (e.g., readiness for learning or prerequisite knowledge) in comparison to their peers are given assistance (e.g., by teaching them basic skills, by filling in knowledge gaps, and the like). On the other hand, the technique of teaching different things to different students consists of *capitalization* inasmuch as the unique strengths of indi-

A. Compensatory techniques

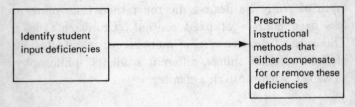

B. Capitalization techniques

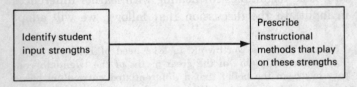

Figure 4.1
Two general techniques for the prescriptive stage of the working model in Figure 2.5

vidual students (e.g., specific aptitudes and interests) are identified and capitalized upon (e.g., by giving them qualitatively different programs of instruction, which may or may not be geared at comparable intellectual levels). With regard to capitalization techniques, the examples already mentioned (vocational schools and elective courses) suggest that different programs of instruction generally result in qualitatively different learned outcomes. However, this does not need to be the case, for capitalization techniques also include approaches whereby different instructional means are used to attain the same or similar instructional goals. Teaching children to read either by the "phonics" or the "whole word" approach represents one example that will be mentioned in this context.

Generally speaking, compensatory techniques in education have been around for some time now in the form of compensatory or remedial programs of instruction, in addition to the tracking philosophy already discussed. Capitalization techniques in education are of more recent vintage, being based on the premise that "different" need not imply anything about "better" or "worse."

Figure 4.2 provides a visual comparison of the traditional approach to schooling and the two prescriptive techniques just described. The notion of *maximization of output* is graphically portrayed in this figure in terms of the number of students who progress from low to high levels of output performance following the implementa-

tion of each technique. Letting $\bigcirc$ and $\square$ repre-

sent different types of students—say roundheads and squareheads, respectively—we see that following the

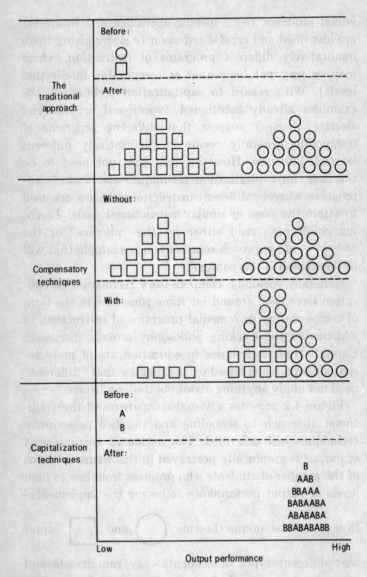

Figure 4.2

A comparison of three types of instructional philosophy

one-for-all instructional treatment of the traditional approach, only the roundheads' performance approaches mastery. At the same time, squareheads are left behind, far short of mastery. These are the dropouts, the ones who could not "make it."

Things look different, however, when we assess output following the implementation of either a compensatory or capitalization technique. In the case of the former, if the squareheads received no effective remedial instruction, the postinstructional result would be the same as with the traditional approach. That is, only the fittest, the roundheads, would survive. With the proper instruction, however, the performance of squareheads is greatly improved. Many even perform at the same level as their roundheaded peers. An even greater degree of output maximization takes place when capitalization techniques are used appropriately. According to this technique, different means of instruction are used to teach unknown material to different types of students, according to their input diagnoses. Thus, students of Type A might receive Instructional Method I and students of Type B might receive Instructional Method II. The end result is that virtually all students attain high levels of mastery.

We shall now present some examples that fit into each technique. However, before we do, we must make a few additional clarifications. In the first place, the compensatory-capitalization distinction should not be regarded as fixed and binding but simply as a general classification aid. This is because in some cases it is difficult to determine whether a particular prescriptive treatment is exclusively compensatory or exclusively capitalization, for it may appear to contain elements of both.

Second, Cronbach and Snow (1976) have broken compensatory techniques down into what they regard as true *compensations* as opposed to *remediations*. With a compensation, the prescriptive path tends to short-circuit a deficiency, whereas with a remediation the prescriptive path consists of removing the deficiency. Consider, for example, a student who lacks some prerequisite skill or ability. On the one hand, we can *compensate* for this deficiency by structuring the target learning materials in such a way that the student is able to succeed despite the deficiency. On the other hand, we can elect not to restructure the learning materials but rather to *remediate* the learner's deficiency so that he will eventually acquire the skill or ability that he presently lacks.

Interestingly, Cronbach and Snow's breakdown of compensatory techniques parallels a similar distinction that others, including myself, have made previously (e.g., Levin, 1972). This distinction involves attempts to improve learning by concentrating either on the *external* or the *internal* side of the learner. If you want to concentrate on the external side, you seek out optimal instructional methods and materials, that is, those that have proven successful in the past. (Note, of course, that what is optimal for one learner may not be optimal for another.) Alternatively, if you want to concentrate on the internal side, you attempt to equip learners with the various learning and problem-solving skills that are related to successful task performance (though these, too may vary from one learner to the next). In the present framework, then, a teacher can strive to maximize learning outputs by improving the quality of either the external props supplied to the learner (i.e., compensation) or the internal mental processes supplied by him (i.e., remediation) (Cronbach and Snow, 1976).

Compensatory Techniques

As you can deduce from Figure 4.2, the basic rationale behind a compensatory approach is to reduce or wipe out output differences that might otherwise result among individuals or groups of individuals. This is accomplished through assisting those individuals who are most in need of assistance. Within this context, the nature of the assistance may vary greatly, from extreme forms of remediation on the one hand to comparatively mild instructional aids on the other. Typically, compensatory techniques incorporated into laboratory experiments are less intense—in terms of the time and effort required to implement them and, therefore, probably in terms of the long-term benefits dervied from them—than those incorporated into educational programs in the classroom.

External Compensatory Techniques. Let us begin by following up on one of the age-related learner difference phenomena described in Chapter 3. You will remember that it has been documented that there is a noticeable shift in the conceptual behavior of children, from an initial proclivity to attend primarily to the physical, perceptible attributes of objects to a later tendency attend to the categorical and functional attributes of the same objects. This shift occurs at about age seven.

In an experiment recently reported by Dr. Linda Ingison and myself (Ingison and Levin, 1975), we tested kindergartners (young children) and sixth graders (older children) on their ability to remember. The experimental task consisted of presenting a child with pictures of common objects, two at a time. In each pair, one of the pictures had a yellow dot beneath it. Later the child was shown the same pairs minus the yellow dot. At this time he simply had to remember which of the two pictures in each pair initially had had a dot beneath it. As might be expected on the basis of our discussion of differences in learning proficiency by age in Chapter 3, the older children mastered the task much more rapidly than the younger children did. However, when we altered the task slightly, we obtained quite different results. In the alternate version, if the yellow dot appeared beneath a particular picture in one pair, it also appeared beneath a perceptually similar picture in a different pair. For example, a picture of a playing card in one pair and a door drawn to the same size and shape in another pair both had yellow dots beneath them. When we used pictures like the door and playing card that possessed perceptible characteristics to which young children are assumed to be well attuned, the younger children mastered the task as quickly as the older children did. What is more, the performance of younger children on the alternate version of the task was as good as that of the older children on the original version.

These data illustrate the operation of a simple *external* compensatory technique. Large differences among learners (here, between learners of different ages) may be reduced substantially when we give assistance to those learners in need of it. In this example, the younger children were given assistance in the form of additional information. But perhaps the results we obtained were due to the possibility that the clues we provided made the task so easy that even a "blockhead" could succeed on it. We ruled out this possibility by repeating the experiment with these same young children, only this time we provided categorical clues (e.g., the yellow dot appeared under a banana and an apple in different pairs). These new clues, however, did not improve their performance. Thus, only when the younger children were provided with clues that were compatible with their input proclivities was performance assisted. This finding has implications for the nature of the compensatory strategies that should be adopted in educational programs. Such strategies must be appropriate in terms of the input characteristics of the students involved if we expect them to be beneficial. We cannot overemphasize the importance of the match between input characteristics and instructional treatments.

Instances of reducing or eliminating age differences by means of appropriate compensatory-type external props abound in the literature. Similarly, reducing group differences, as defined in terms of other learner input variables, are also easy to identify. Fuller (1974), for example, has described a novel technique for teaching otherwise nonreading low IQ students to read, a technique that has been found to reduce dramatically the existing decoding and comprehension differences between high and low IQ students. The method consists of forming all the upper case letters of the alphabet using only three symbols—a line, a circle, and an angle—each with a unique color. The sounds the letters make are emphasized prior to their names, and almost immediately students are given words and sentences to read in the context of exciting stories. Initial evaluations of the method have revealed phenomenal successes. Having poor readers listen to (rather than read) information is another compensatory technique that has proven successful in improving their comprehension (Lundsteen, 1971).

Internal Compensatory Techniques. Analogous evidence can be marshalled in support of compensatory techniques of the *internal* variety, where the emphasis is on what the learner can be taught to do for himself (i.e., in terms of his own mental activity) rather than what others can do for him (i.e., in terms of external props). In our own research, we have found that the reading comprehension of certain poor readers can be greatly improved if they are first instructed in the use of effective comprehension strategies. One strategy requires the reader to pause after each sentence to construct a mental picture of the information it contains and then to relate the pictures in one sentence to those in the next. As he does this, the reader gives a compact organizational structure to the passage. Numerous experiments have been conducted that demonstrate ways in which differences in learning proficiency can be reduced through learners' use of appropriate internal mental processes like the imagery strategy just described (Levin, 1976).

In the same vein, if it can be shown that certain intellectual styles or strategy classifications are related positively or negatively to learning outputs, then we should use this information in prescribing remedial treatments. For example, if "reflective" children turn out to be better learners, we could experiment to find out whether simply slowing down "impulsive" children improves their learning (e.g., Bender, 1976). Certainly this suggestion would be compatible with Carroll's (1963) belief that the amount of time effectively spent in learning is a crucial variable. Similarly, if children who prefer one basis for classification are inefficient learners (e.g., Yussen, Levin, DeRose, and Ghatala, 1976), we could instruct them in alternative bases for classification. Or we could follow an external compensatory technique and restructure the learning materials to *match* their individual preferences, as in the Ingison and Levin (1975) experiment described earlier (see also Ramirez and Casteñada, 1974.)*

To summarize, even though many individuals fail to employ efficient modes of learning in their day-to-day encounters, they might be able to become more efficient through appropriate kinds of instruction or training. We have seen illustrations of this philosophy on a micro level. Let us now examine it briefly on a macro level.

Educational programs incorporating compensatory strategies. Clearly, most of the large-scale educational programs designed to maximize output have adopted a compensatory-technique approach. (As we shall see shortly, some of the more recent individualized programs also make use of capitalization techniques.) The tracking system, which we mentioned earlier, is truly compensatory in that it is based on the evaluation of students in terms of general ability *levels* (high versus low, as in our roundhead-squarehead examples) rather than in terms of specific ability *differences* (Ability A versus Ability B, where the two abilities may represent quite different dimensions).

This has certainly been true of the much-publicized remedial education programs of recent years. Project Head Start was designed to provide lower-class children with some of the learning experiences and skills that they were assumed to be lacking, in an attempt to reduce the prerequisite gap in terms of readiness for schooling between such children and those from middle-class

---

* It is worth noting, however, that relationships of this kind are often attributable to variables behind the scene, i.e., to variables of which we are unaware. Because of this, dealing with the visible symptoms (rather than the invisible causes) may not always yield the desired result.

homes, who were likely to acquire relevant learning experiences and skills through their normal day-to-day encounters. A similar rationale lay behind the development of the popular *Sesame Street* television program. Although evidence of gap-closing, especially long-term evidence, has not been apparent from such programs (Cook, 1974; Jensen, 1969), there is no question that they have provided lower-class children with a variety of educational experiences that they otherwise would not have had.

Two highly successful federally funded educational programs are Individually Prescribed Instruction (IPI), which was begun at the University of Pittsburgh, and Individually Guided Education (IGE), initiated at the University of Wisconsin. Both these programs contain compensatory techniques among their principal ingredients. To date, one of IPIs distinctions has been to use a computer-managed system to deal with student input differences (Cooley and Glaser, 1969; Hambleton, 1974). We will look at the basic advantages of computers with regard to individualization of instruction later in this chapter. IGE, on the other hand, has dealt with learner differences by abandoning the traditional age-grade classroom arrangement in favor of small units and specially designed curricular materials, which are used in conjunction with students' input profiles. Unit leaders work closely with students exhibiting similar profiles in various skill areas (in particular, reading and mathematics), prescribing the appropriate instructional and/or remedial lessons that may be required (Klausmeier, 1971). Currently, numerous target schools across the country are participating in individualized programs such as these.

Capitalization Techniques

From these examples you can see that the intent of compensatory techniques is to provide *more* assistance to learners who have *less* of something (e.g., less intellectual development or less in the way of prerequisite skills). With capitalization techniques, however, the assumption is that even though two learners are at comparable *general* intellectual levels, they may nonetheless possess quite different patterns of *specific* abilities and aptitudes. Differences of this sort were described in our earlier discussion of intellectual styles and strategies in Chapter 3. For instance, given two learners of the same age and with identical IQs, one of them may prefer— and may be better at—processing verbal information auditorily (through listening) and the other visually (through reading); or one may prefer to process information rapidly, attending only to global characteristics of incoming stimuli or to general concepts, while the other may prefer to be more deliberate in processing information, attending to highly specific details. (Refer back to our twin example in Chapter 1 for evidence of marked differences in social style between otherwise comparable individuals.)

Given the finding that such different preferred modes of information processing exist among learners, you should find it easy to understand why a traditional approach to schooling is doomed to failure. At best, it can work only for some of the students some of the time. In other words, lacking information about individuals' intellectual styles and strategies—or being aware of their existence but not capitalizing on them—the teacher will not be able to maximize learning for all of the students all of the time. When a unit of instruction is presented in a single mode and at a single pace, many students will experience discrepancies between their own *optimal* instructional vehicles and the *actual* ones employed.

The research of Pask and Scott (1972) provides an example of how it is possible to capitalize on learners' strengths in order to prescribe an appropriate means of instruction. As we mentioned in Chapter 3, Pask and his associates have identified two general classes of prose learners—*serialists*, who tend to remember prose material in terms of simple data links, and *holists*, who tend to remember higher order relationships within the material. According to this distinction, serialists are typically found to be "intolerant of irrelevant information [Pask and Scott, 1972, p. 218]," whereas holists tend to incorporate all of the basic facts and details into their general scheme of things.

In their experiment with college students, Pask and Scott were able to identify serialist and holist types on the basis of an initial "free-learning" session in which the students were allowed to select cards and ask questions relevant to the acquisition of information about a fictitious animal species. The complexity of the questions generated by a student dictated whether he fit the serialist or the holist mold. Following this initial task, the students were given a unit of instruction about a different species, but this time they were required to study one of two prearranged passages or programs. One of these had been designed to benefit serialist types, in that it presented the information in a straightforward, no-nonsense fashion. The other had been designed to benefit holist types, in that lots of details (some relevant) and pictures representing various concepts were provided, along with several potentially interesting—for holists

—informational asides. According to Pask and Scott, "Both . . . convey exactly the same *strictly relevant* information, knowledge of which is *subsequently tested* . . . But the concepts they instruct are different and very differently structured [p. 239]."

In the experiment, students were either "matched" or "mismatched" in terms of the program they were presented. Matched students were given the program that was designed for students of their type. That is, a serialist student was given the serialist program, and a holist student was given the holist program. Mismatched students were given the program that was designed for students of the other type. Pask and Scott found that when students and programs were matched, learning (as assessed on a 30-item test) was clearly superior to that obtained when students and programs were mismatched. All matched students (both serialists and holists) correctly answered at least 28 out of 30 questions on the test, while mismatched students answered only 7 to 21 questions correctly.

This study reveals in dramatic fashion the essence of a capitalization technique. When the input strengths of learners were identified and capitalized upon, subsequent learning was very efficient. When these strengths were not capitalized upon, learning was not as efficient. While evidence as clear or as convincing as this may not always be so easy to come by, it is apparent that an increasing number of educators and psychologists are beginning to take capitalization techniques seriously. One evidence of this is the widespread attention being given to the "aptitude-by-treatment interaction" or ATI movement in recent years (Berliner and Cahen, 1973).

The notion that different instructional treatments are called for when dealing with learners of differing input strengths or aptitudes is what capitalization techniques are all about. The simplest instance of an ATI occurs in the situation depicted in Figure 4.3, in which one of two treatments is administered to learners of one of two aptitude types. This graph shows that learners of the same type can demonstrate quite different performances as a function of the particular instructional treatment received. Type A learners (for instance, serialists in our previous example) will perform well if given Treatment I (the serialist program) but not if given Treatment II (the holist program). On the other hand, Type B learners (holists) will succeed with Treatment II but

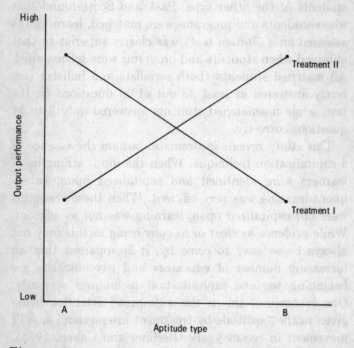

Figure 4.3
Example of an aptitude by treatment interaction (ATI)

not with Treatment I. Thus, our task as educators is to match aptitude types with instructional treatments that are known or believed to be appropriate for learners of that type. Successful matches should produce a maximization of output, as represented in the bottom panel of Figure 4.2.

One ATI that seems especially relevant to reading instruction for young children was cited by Cronbach and Snow (1969). It consisted of demonstrating a relationship between modality preferences of children (visual versus auditory) and their ability to profit from phonics or whole-word instructional approaches to reading. As predicted, children with high auditory aptitudes learned to read better when a phonics approach, which emphasized sounds, was followed. In contrast, children with high visual aptitudes learned to read better with a whole-word approach, which emphasized visual configurations (Bissell, White, and Zivin, 1971). It should be noted, however, that not all results in this domain have been positive (Ysseldyke, 1973). Other examples of interesting ATIs, including ones with implications for learning in school, may be found in Cronbach and Snow (1976).

Researchers have also looked into the area of matching teacher and student intellectual styles and strategies. As one example, the amount of structure preferred or required by students and the amount provided by the teacher during instruction have been found to interact in the manner prescribed by Figure 4.3 (Kogan, 1971; Witkin, 1973).

Certainly the present discussion of ATIs represents an idealized view. In reality the implementation of an ATI technique in the classroom is not an easy task. In the first place, aptitudes are often difficult to identify.

In most cases the identification of student aptitudes requires thoughtful analyses of behavior and/or performance on psychometrically sound (i.e., reliable and valid) measuring instruments. (In this regard it should be mentioned that standardized instruments for assessing various aptitudes have been developed and are on the market.) Similarly, the potential relationship between a particular aptitude and a desired output must be more than a casual possibility. It is probably not very informative, for example, to know that a student has high numerical ability when prescribing a particular instructional treatment for an art lesson. (Perhaps it would be relevant for some aspects of art such as "perspective" and "balance" but in general, a relationship between the two is not obvious.)

In the same vein, some knowledge must also be available concerning treatments. That is, which treatments are likely to work with learners of a given aptitude? On the surface this may not seem to be a difficult question, but to date researchers have produced few clues and no definitive answers. The problem is complicated further by the likelihood that different aptitude-treatment combinations are called for in different subject matter areas or even for different subject matter content within the same general area.

Finally, as we saw in Chapter 3, few learning outputs can be traced to a single input variable. More often, input variable complexes are associated with output. So, to prescribe treatments based on single aptitude identifications is not likely to be as productive as we might hope. Extensions of the ATI technique to multiple aptitudes—along the lines of the two input variable case in Figure 3.2—appear to be both worthwhile and possible endeavors, given the increased sophistication of modern-day educational technology.

Learner Differences: Recent Instructional Approaches

Traces of both compensatory and capitalization techniques may be found in the more recent attempts to deal with learner differences in the classroom. The traditional approach to schooling is beginning to give way to a situation in which the needs and goals of individual students are being considered. Moreover, unlike the initial approaches for coping with existing differences (i.e., where students are segregated on the basis of their age, ability, or vocational plans), more basic elements of the traditional classroom instructional arrangement are being challenged. No longer is the traditional classroom structure viewed as fixed and unchangeable, nor is the teacher seen as the sole, or even the primary, dispenser of knowledge. In considering recent approaches based on this new philosophy, we shall discuss first those that can be related to technological advances and second those that can be related to humanistic concerns.

Learner Differences and Technological Advances

The most popularized version of *individualized instruction* has its roots in the efforts to deal with learner differences in the *rate*, *sequence*, and *nature* of materials required or desired during a unit of instruction (Skinner, 1968). Initially, mechanical teaching machines and textbooks with *linear programs* were introduced to allow a student to proceed through a unit of instruction at a rate that was comfortable for him. Hopefully, this would prevent a student from becoming lost or bored, the way that he might when following a teacher presenting a lesson at a rate that was too fast or slow.

In *programmed instruction* students are given a unit of instruction in small pieces, called *frames*, which typically contain one or two sentences for the student to read. The student may take as long as he wishes to read and review each frame, but usually he must demonstrate mastery of its content before he is permitted to continue to the next frame. Should a student make errors anywhere in the program, he may be "recycled" to the particular instructional content causing him problems. However, such errors are unlikely since the material is presented in very small pieces and mastery assessment and feedback are immediate. The effectiveness of this approach in terms of output maximization is assumed to reside in the scientific principles underlying the *shaping technique* associated with *operant conditioning*. Thus, programmed instruction is a process that involves active participation of a learner progressing in such small steps that a virtually errorless performance results. When these responses are followed by immediate feedback (*reinforcement*), this is assumed to strengthen the responses (Reese, 1976).

Next came a consideration of sequence differences. *Branching programs* permitted learners with different input characteristics and different on-line learning experiences (i.e., different degrees of success while progressing through the program) to arrive at the same place through a variety of routes. Thus, a student with a great deal of prerequisite knowledge related to the instructional material presented (as determined, perhaps, by a pretest at the beginning of the program) might be able to take a shorter route through the program, skipping those frames that present the prerequisite knowledge, which a student lacking that knowledge would be required to read. Similarly, a student who experiences no difficulties as he progresses could take a different route from the student who is unsure of himself or who makes occasional mistakes. For example, the latter student might be routed to auxiliary material designed to expand upon or clarify the material causing him problems.

As you can see, the programmed instruction systems we have presented thus far have contained compensatory components. Students requiring more time or different paths of instruction are accommodated. The rationale behind such programmed instruction is similar to that behind the tracking system where students of comparable ability levels are placed in the same classroom. However, there is one distinguishing characteristic of the tracking system. All students within the same track receive instruction from the teacher in a more or less traditional manner (i.e., one rate, one sequence). This does not occur with a programmed instruction format, for each student within a classroom can proceed at his own pace, covering material that has been deemed appropriate for him. In addition, programmed instruction provides a system in which sequence decisions are preprogrammed and depend only on students' responses. Thus the system does something a teacher cannot, for what single human being could keep track of the individual responses of 20 or 30 children and then prescribe individualized paths of instruction on the basis of particular needs?

The capabilities of programmed instruction, as described up to this point, were those that existed before the computer. However, now that the computer age is upon us, Hal and his friends have opened up possibilities that only Stanley Kubrick could have dreamed of! Indeed, programmed textbooks and mechanical teaching machines pale in comparison to what can be accomplished through the electronic computers of today.

On the instructional side of the coin, computers have been recruited to teach subject matter to students—from basic reading skills in the primary grades to college-level courses in logic and statistics. On the diagnostic-prescriptive side, these same computers can be programmed to gather all kinds of input and throughput data in order to make appropriate instructional content and sequence decisions for individual students.*

Clearly most of these decisions are of the compensatory variety. For example, if the student is doing poorly, additional instruction via a remedial route may be prescribed. However, capitalization techniques are also able to be incorporated. That is, following diagnoses of a student's characteristic intellectual styles and strategies, materials compatible with his strengths and preferences can be presented. We can even program our computers to be "compassionate" inasmuch as individualized instructional goals may be considered. Grubb (1969), for example, has described a computer-based system for teaching statistics in a manner that accommodates students who are taking the course with very different objectives in mind. Other impressive illustrations of what has been accomplished in the brief history of computers in education may be found in various

---

* Contrary to popular belief, we (the educators) are still in control of the kinds of data that are fed into computers and, consequently, the kinds of prescriptions that computers read out.

sources—although by the time you read these accounts, they probably will be outdated (Atkinson and Wilson, 1969).

Learner Differences and Humanistic Concerns

Grubb's (1969) computerized manner of prescribing different instructional content for students with different instructional goals surely represents an attempt to deal with humanistic concerns in education. Specifically, the student is given a choice regarding what he wants to learn—an approach that caters to each individual's objectives when prescribing instructional content. However, in Grubb's system—as in the elective and vocational programs mentioned earlier—once this specification is made, how the student learns is no longer in his own hands. Rather, the computer, or the teacher, then takes over. However, certain alternatives to the traditional approach have leaned in the direction of extending the student choice thesis to its logical conclusion by encouraging the student to choose not merely his instructional goals but his instructional means as well.

For example, with the so-called *open-classroom* approach (which contains elements of the much-publicized *Summerhill* program of A. S. Neill, 1960), the teacher is viewed as a facilitator of individualized goals, but one who does not define the subject matter content or dictate the instructional means related to its attainment. To the contrary, the student learns what he wants to learn how and when he wants to learn it. The teacher makes available to each student a rich assortment of educational materials such as books, filmstrips, and games, which are sometimes assembled together in *learning centers* (Waynant and Wilson, 1974). A teacher may also provide educational experiences such as demonstrations, experiments, and field trips. Moreover, supplementary information and encouragement are given to individual children if and when the need arises (Kohl, 1969).

The Wisconsin IGE system includes aspects of this philosophy. For example, unit leaders are seen as facilitators of individual rather than group goals. Moreover, the implementation of a subsystem known as *individually guided motivation* permits each student to establish to some extent, his own learning objectives—both by nature and number (Klausmeier et al., 1975).

However, as is true with most of the contemporary learner difference efforts discussed in this chapter, even though the philosophy of the open classroom carries a good deal of intuitive appeal, we do not yet know how effective a philosophy it is for learning. We do not yet have scientifically sound data assessing the comparative intellectual, attitudinal, and emotional developments of students given a free hand in selecting their learning goals and means and those educated along more traditional lines.

Following Prescription, What Then?

We have now reached the final stage (#6) in our Figure 2.5 model. This stage calls for continual evaluation and reevaluation of diagnoses and prescriptions. Were our diagnoses accurate? Were our prescriptions successful? If not, why not? What alternative methods could we prescribe?

Many of our diagnoses will be in error (remember the

issue of reliability) as will many of our prescriptions. With regard to prescriptions, we know that (1) designated input variables may not be related to output in the anticipated manner (remember validity); (2) selected treatments may not interact with input variables in the manner we had hoped, according to an ATI stance; and/or (3) there are learner input variables apart from the one(s) we may have considered (motivation to learn, for example) that are operating against us.

Hopefully, we will not be discouraged by such setbacks. Despite occasional detractors (e.g., Gage and Unruh, 1967), the rationale behind individually tailored approaches to schooling is a sound one and one that is currently in need of all the optimism and resources we can throw its way. Now that we have presented the components of Figure 2.5, I still hear you asking, "Can we, the current generation of teachers in America, pull it off; or are these diagnoses and prescriptions related to abstract theory rather than to real live children in actual classrooms?" The answer to that question is both yes and no.

Yes, in that if the initial signs are accurate, individualized school programs such as IPI and IGE offer encouragement. These programs demonstrate that greater individualization of classroom instruction is certainly plausible, and not at the expense of vast resources or superhuman efforts on the parts of teachers and staffs. Indeed, with respect to implementing the IGE system, Klausmeier (1971) prescribes the following minimal requisites:

Allocate at least $10 per pupil during the first two years for any combination of one instructional aide per

150 children, additional instructional materials, and higher pay for the lead teacher. Title I or Title III funds should be available for this.

Remodel the "eggcrate" type school building so that there will be one well-supplied instructional resource center to accommodate at least 90 intermediate-age children and another center to accommodate at least 60 primary-age children. Local funds should be available for the remodeling and Title I, II, or III funds for the materials and equipment.

Participate in a staff development program starting with a one-day workshop for chief school officers, a three-day workshop for the prospective building principal and unit leaders of the various [schools], a one-week workshop for the entire staff of each [school] prior to the opening of the [school] in the fall (this may be spread out during a semester), four half-day workshops for the entire staff of each building during the first year, and a one-week institute for central office consultants in the curriculum area which will be given most attention during the first year. Here the local school should pay time and travel expenses of its personnel and the state educational agency should provide its staff to lead all the workshops except the one which occurs prior to the opening of the school. This is staffed by the local school district. In Wisconsin the Department of Public Instruction and local school districts have been implementing this program since 1968 [p. 184].

On the other hand, the answer is no in that reasonable diagnoses and prescriptions need not be an unmanageable task for the typical classroom teacher. Thus, suppose, that your school or school district has neither the resources nor the inclination to invest in large-scale individualized programs of the kind just described. Can you still behave in the spirit of the Figure 2.5 model? I certainly think you can. In Chapter 5 we will examine how a teacher in a typical classroom can conduct an educational activity according to our model.

Suggested Readings

Bruner, J. S. *The process of education*. New York: Vintage, 1960.

Carroll, J. A model of school learning. *Teachers College Record*, 1963, **64**, 723–733.

Cooley, W. W., & Glaser, R. An information and management system for individually prescribed instruction. In R. C. Atkinson and H. A. Wilson (Eds.), *Computer-assisted instruction: A book of readings*. New York: Academic Press, 1969.

Fuller, R. Breaking down the IQ walls: Severely retarded people *can* learn to read. *Psychology Today*, 1974, **8**, 96–102.

Gage, N. L., & Unruh, W. R. Theoretical formulations for research on teaching. *Review of Educational Research*, 1967, **37**, 358–370.

Gagné, R. M. *Essentials of learning for instruction*. New York: Holt, Rinehart and Winston, 1974.

Glaser, R. Individuals and learning: The new aptitudes. *Educational Researcher*, 1972, **1** (6), 5–13.

Grubb, R. E. Learner-controlled statistics. In R. C. Atkinson & H. A. Wilson (Eds.), *Computer-assisted instruction: A book of readings*. New York: Academic Press, 1969.

Klausmeier, H. J. The multi-unit elementary school and individually guided education. *Phi Delta Kappan*, Nov. 1971, 181–184.

Kohl, H. R. *The open classroom*. New York: Vintage, 1969.

Lesser, G. S. Matching instruction to student characteristics. In G. S. Lesser (Ed.), *Psychology and educational practice*. Glenview, Ill.: Scott, Foresman and Co., 1971a.

Levin, J. R. What have we learned about maximizing what children learn? In J. R. Levin & V. L. Allen (Eds.), *Cognitive learning in children: Theories and strategies*. New York: Academic Press, 1976.

Neill, A. S. *Summerhill: A radical approach to child rearing*. New York: Hart, 1960.

Ramirez, M. III, Casteñada, A. *Cultural democracy, bicognitive development, and education*. New York: Academic Press, 1974.

Reese, H. W. *Basic learning processes in childhood*. New York: Holt, Rinehart and Winston, 1976.

Skinner, B. F. *The technology of teaching*. New York: Appleton-Century-Crofts, 1968.

Waynant, L. F., & Wilson, R. M. *Learning centers . . . A guide for effective use*. Paoli, Pa.: Instructo Corp., 1974.

Ysseldyke, J. E. Diagnostic-prescriptive teaching: The search for aptitude-treatment interactions. In L. Mann & D. A. Sabatino (Eds.), *The first review of special education*. Philadelphia: JSE Press, 1973.

Chapter 5   Implementing the Model

In the following discussion we will focus on reading achievement as an output variable of interest, since (1) it is a variable that is easy for most of us to relate to; (2) we have used it as an example throughout this book; and (3) there currently exist reasonable diagnostic-prescriptive offerings in this domain. Let us, therefore, go through the six steps of our model (see Figure 2.5) with the objective of maximizing students' reading achievement.

Individualizing Reading Instruction: An Example

Step 1: Observe Output Differences

By now it should come as no surprise to you that the students within almost any given classroom will vary considerably in the extent to which they can acquire information from a printed page (i.e., comprehend what they read). Moreover, this is true both in the early grades, where students with different background experiences embark on the reading process with different prerequisite skills more or less developed, and in the later grades. Many of these reader differences are visible to the observant teacher. That is, we can usually distinguish between the good and poor readers as a result of our day-to-day classroom encounters with these students. However, for reasons already discussed in Chapters 2 and 3, we may have to back up impressions of this kind concerning reader differences with other evidence. Because our observations may be somewhat unreliable and/or invalid (sometimes as a result of their being colored by our subjective stereotypes and expectations), we would do well to combine them with additional sources of data.

Let us say that we select a standardized measure of reading achievement such as the comprehension subtest of the Stanford Achievement Test or that of the Iowa Test of Basic Skills. The reliabilities of these measures are well established and respectable. Specifically, they have reliabilities in the .80s, which indicates that repeated assessments using these instruments tend to be very consistent. In addition, these tests have been found to be reasonably valid predictors of reading achievement as determined on the basis of other criteria.

It is worth noting here, however, that despite the general validity of these group-administered tests, the validity of a test score obtained by a particular student may occasionally be questioned by a teacher. I have frequently heard teachers remark, for example, that Johnny is a very good reader despite what his low score on the standardized reading test says. A teacher may remember noticing that Johnny was fooling around on the day the test was administered, or that he had been permitted to leave the room and was unable to finish all the questions when he returned. Obviously in such cases, it would be foolhardy to ignore other evidence (e.g., in-class observations) concerning Johnny's reading ability.

In situations where proper test administration conditions (including motivational components) have been achieved, the scores on these reading achievement tests may be taken as fairly valid indices of students' reading abilities. The *grade equivalent scores* achieved on such tests can be used to identify those students who are reading at a "normal" level for students in their grade and those students who are reading above or below "normal" levels. Thus, on the basis of the standardized test (combined, perhaps, with other pertinent in-class data), we are able to diagnose which students are below "normal" levels and are in need of some type of remediation. However, because poor reading achievement undoubtedly results from more than one cause, we will have to dig more deeply before we can hope to come up with appropriate prescriptions for particular students.

Step 2: Ask "Why?"

Having noted that some of our students are reading at or above grade level whereas others are reading below grade level, we might be prompted to ask what causes these differences. Invariably the answer to this question involves a knowledge of—or an assumption about—the constituent skills involved in the output variable of interest. In the present example, before attempting to understand the causes of differences in students' reading achievement, we must first attempt to define the behavioral components involved in the act of reading itself. In other words, some type of task analysis (see the Gagné, 1974, volume in this series) of the reading process is required. Such an analysis might resemble the "armchair" version proposed in Figure 5.1.

According to this representation, in order for a student to be able to read with comprehension, it is assumed that he must possess a set of hierarchically ordered subordinate skills or subskills. Starting from the bottom of Figure 5.1, each subskill is assumed to be a necessary but not sufficient component of the next higher reading subskill. Thus, if a student does not attend to the symbols, he will not be able to decode the words. If he does not decode the words, he will not derive meanings from them, and so forth. (Note that if, in addition, we wanted to determine whether a particular student reads with comprehension, we would have to include a box at the very top of the hierarchy representing the student's ability to demonstrate comprehension by means of some type of performance, either verbal or nonverbal.)

We can translate this task analysis into a series of questions that we can then use to determine whether a particular student possesses all the necessary subskills required to read proficiently and, if not, which specific subskills he appears to lack. Fortunately, a recent discussion of various assumed causes of reading difficulty corresponds nicely with the questions suggested by the

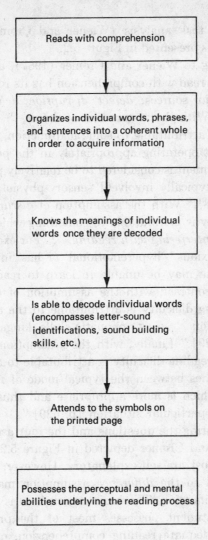

Figure 5.1
Task analysis of the process of reading with comprehension

Figure 5.1 task analysis (Wiener and Cromer, 1967). The result is presented in Figure 5.2.

According to Wiener and Cromer (1967), a student's inability to read with comprehension has its roots in one of four major sources: *defect, disruption, deficiency,* or *difference.* With the assumption of *defect,* ". . . reading difficulty is attributable to some malfunction, i.e., something is not operating appropriately in the person. . . . This impairment is considered to be relatively permanent . . . [and typically involves] sensory-physiological factors [p. 628]." With the assumption of *disruption,* ". . . the difficulty is attributable to something which is *present* but is *interfering with reading.* . . . For example, if a child is 'anxious,' 'hyperemotional' or has 'intrapsychic conflicts,' he may be unable to learn to read . . . [p. 629]." In contrast, with the assumption of *deficiency,* ". . . reading difficulty is attributable to the *absence* of some function . . . (e.g., phonetic skills, language skills, etc.) [p. 629]." Finally, with the assumption of *difference,* ". . . reading difficulty is attributable to *differences* or mismatches between the typical mode of responding and that which is more appropriate and thus the best payoff in a particular situation [p. 629]."

In comparing the questions and the four assumptions of Wiener and Cromer depicted in Figure 5.2, you will find that most are self-explanatory. However, the question related to the *difference* assumption may require further clarification. The basic notion here is that even though a student possesses most of the prerequisite skills for adequate reading comprehension, one reason why he may still read poorly is because his characteristic way of grouping together words, phrases, and sentences is insufficient for him to derive meaning from them. These poor organizational or synthesis skills

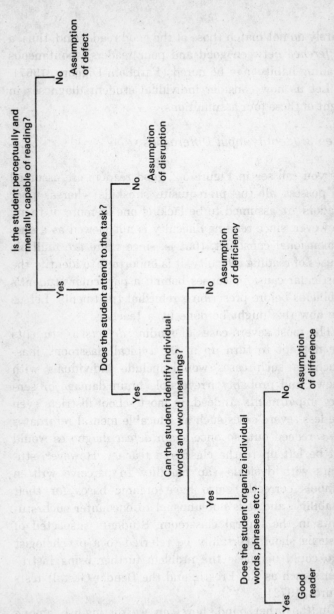

Figure 5.2 Translation of Figure 5.1's task analysis into a set of questions

surely do not match those of the good reader and, thus, a *difference* between good and poor readers' spontaneous reading habits may be noted (Farnham-Diggory, 1967).

Let us now consider individual student diagnoses in light of these four assumptions.

Step 3: Identify Input Differences

As you can see in Figure 5.2, good readers are assumed to possess all the prerequisite subskills whereas poor readers are assumed to be lacking one or more of them. However, since reading difficulty is not viewed as a one-dimensional construct, that is, since there are multiple causes of reading difficulty, it is important to identify the particular cause or causes behind a particular student's problems before prescribing remedial treatments. Let us see how this might be done by a teacher.

The most severe cases of reading *defects* in students are not apt to turn up in the typical classroom, inasmuch as such cases would include individuals with known and probably irreversible brain damage or sensory impairments. Indeed, in most school districts even the less severe cases such as educable mental retardates are screened out, so once again *defect* diagnoses would not be left up to the classroom teacher. However, students with dyslexia (an inability to perceive written symbols correctly) also have organic bases for their disability, and it is not unusual to encounter such students in the typical classroom. Students suspected of dyslexia should certainly be referred to a psychologist who could diagnose the problem further using instruments such as the Frostig and the Bender-Gestalt tests (Buros, 1972).

On the other hand, how can we distinguish among

poor-reading students whose problems may be attributable primarily to *disruptions, deficiencies,* or *differences*? Suggestions of a *disruption*-related cause will probably come from a teacher's observations of a student's characteristic in-class behavior or study activity. As Wiener and Cromer (1967) noted, anxiety or hyper-emotionality may be pertinent behavioral traits to consider (as might be hyperactivity—recall the description of Twin B in Chapter 1). Similarly, tests of intellectual style, like those referred to in Chapter 3, might be used to diagnose children who typically are "impulsive" or who are easily distracted by extraneous stimuli (Kogan, 1971).

Deficiencies, as primary cases for reading failures, are probably the easiest to diagnose. If a child is given a series of letters and cannot identify their associated names or sounds, then that child would be assumed to have a letter-sound identification deficiency. Similarly, if he cannot blend letter sounds properly to form words, he would be exhibiting a word decoding deficiency. (Finer breakdowns of word decoding skills are used by those concerned with the acquisition of prereading skills —Samuels, forthcoming.) Alternatively, suppose a student is able to sound out and pronounce individual words correctly, but he does not know the meaning of the word once pronounced because it is foreign to his vocabulary. Clearly this student has a vocabulary deficiency that limits the extent of his reading comprehension or, for that matter, his listening comprehension. Particular deficiencies might therefore be diagnosed on the basis of specific tests administered by. the teacher (e.g., letter-sound identification tests, word reading tests, and/or vocabulary tests) most of which are available in standardized form.

Finally, students assumed to be reading poorly as a result of *differences* might be identified by the process of elimination. That is, if they do not seem to exhibit any of the problems we have just described, but they still have difficulty comprehending what they read, a *difference* problem might be suspected. One way to test whether this is due to a lack of synthesis would be to have the student read aloud. Comparing the way in which words and phrases should be grouped together with the way a student actually groups them can provide clues to the source of his poor comprehension. In like manner, the student's inflections and attention to punctuation cues may also provide evidence.

The preceding discussion was not meant to be exhaustive, but it is representative of the kinds of leads a teacher might follow in order to diagnose specific reading comprehension problems. Psychologists and reading specialists can help you by suggesting other possible leads. The important point is that until the source of the poor reader's problem is identified, at least to some extent, you cannot take a reasonable prescriptive path. As we shall see in the following section, the particular path may vary considerably from one student to the next.

Step 4: "What Can Be Done?"

In order to make the following discussion more concrete, let us return to some old acquaintances:

As may be seen in Figure 2.1, these nine students from our hypothetical classroom are the ones who may be regarded as below-average readers. Based on individual

Table 5.1

Diagnoses and Prescriptions for the Nine Below-Average
Readers in Figure 2.1

Student	Diagnosis		Prescription
	General	*Specific*	
	Deficiency	Inadequate letter-sound knowledge	Teach letter-sound identification skills
	Disruption	Anxious	Provide information in alternative modes
	Disruption	Unmotivated	Provide incentives
	Deficiency	Inadequate vocabulary knowledge	Provide materials with simpler vocabulary
	Deficiency	Cannot decode	Teach decoding skills
	Disruption	Easily distracted	Increase interest level of the materials
	Difference	Improper synthesis	Provide materials with simpler structure
	Deficiency	Inadequate vocabulary knowledge	Expand existing vocabulary
	Difference	Improper synthesis	Teach synthesis skills

diagnoses, suppose we come up with classifications such
as the ones presented in Table 5.1. It will be noted that

each below-average reader has been further diagnosed according to Wiener-Cromer (1967) symptoms, at both a general and a more specific level.

Let us consider the general diagnoses first. (In this example we have proceeded as though no students with mental and sensory *defects* are part of the classroom. Accordingly, reading difficulty is assumed to result primarily from *disruptions*, *deficiencies*, or *differences*.) Based on specific diagnoses of individual students, we note that three students seem to fall into the disruption category ([icon] , [icon] , and [icon] , with evidences of anxiety, lack of motivation, and distractibility, respectively). Similarly, four students ([icon] , [icon] , [icon] , and [icon]) appear to exhibit a basic deficiency; and two ([icon] and [icon]), a difference.

What can we do in the way of prescribing instructional treatments of the compensatory variety to make these students better readers? The final column in Table 5.1 includes some possible prescriptions. These prescriptions come from specific treatments that in the past have tended to work for students with similar symptoms.

Take the case of poor ☹ , a student with little or no motivation to learn to read. Based on a sampling of the motivation and reinforcement literature in education and psychology, we might discover that certain kinds of incentives seem to work well for students with a lack of motivation similar to ☹ 's. In particular, we might find that tangible reinforcers like candy work especially well for ☹ in this particular context. In different contexts or for different individuals, on the other hand, certain social reinforcers, such as verbal praise, may be more effective. Determining the appropriate match among individuals, contexts, and reinforcers is an important, though often formidable, task (Baer, forthcoming).

Now contrast the case of ☹ with that of ☹ . Reading makes ☹ feel very anxious and upset. Possibly reading has become an aversive experience for

⊠ , for any number of reasons. To alleviate some of her anxiety, it might be desirable to shape ⊠ 's attitude toward learning in a particular curricular area by first having her learn through alternative modes or media that she has found enjoyable in the past. For instance, listening to presented information or watching educational slides or films might be appropriate initial vehicles. Subsequently, ⊠ might follow along in a book while her teacher reads aloud, or she might attempt to read stories combined with pictures representing their content. The basic notion here is initially to compensate for ⊠ 's anxiety associated with reading by using alternative modes of information dissemination.

A similar prescription may be made for ☺ , the student who is easily distracted. Is he distracted because he is bored with the usual reading materials he receives? If so, providing him with something more interesting

(i.e., more in line with his personal tastes and preferences) may be indicated. Certain apparent "nonreaders"
can be magically transformed into "readers" once the
Dicks and Janes become Bonnies and Clydes or some
other intriguing characters (Fuller, 1974). Indeed, some
of the recent successes in motivating lower-class children
through the use of popular paperback books, sports
stories in the newspapers, and the like are founded on
this assumption (Fader and McNeil, 1968).

The prescriptions in the case of the four *deficiency*
students in Table 5.1 appear straightforward. However,
let us compare alternative prescriptions for two students
with the same diagnosed deficiency (i.e., for [😦] and
[🙂] , both of whom have underdeveloped vocabularies). On the one hand, we may elect to prescribe reading
materials that contain simpler vocabulary items than
those currently provided. Such a prescription might be

of benefit in the short term, in that ☹ might begin reading almost immediately, something that might be necessary to increase her self-confidence. On the other hand, we may elect to bolster the student's existing vocabulary through an arduous program of instruction and practice. Adhering to a long-term remediation philosophy, we might choose this course of action for 😐 .

It is worth pointing out that these two alternative prescriptions for the same problem may be looked at in terms of the external-internal compensatory technique distinction referred to in Chapter 4. You will recall that with external compensatory techniques, the basic idea is to restructure the learning environment to make things easier for the learner. This is what we chose to do for ☹ , a student with a poor vocabulary. We simply gave her materials to read that were easier than those typically provided, that is, we compensated for her deficiency.

With [image: icon] , however, we opted for a compensatory technique of the internal variety. The basic idea with this technique is to place the burden on the learner, that is, to equip him with the skills required for successful independent performance (i.e., to remediate his deficiency). This is what we hope to accomplish by taking [image: icon] through a vocabulary-improvement program.

The same external-internal distinction may be applied to the prescriptions for the two students in Table 5.1 with *difference* problems. For one of them, [image: icon] , we might attempt to overcome his synthesis difficulties by simplifying the structure of the reading materials. This is an external technique, and in this context it might consist of providing reading materials with fewer words per idea unit and/or less complex grammatical structures. Thus, two- or three-word sentences might supplant seven- or eight-word sentences. With reduced sentence lengths, 🙂 would be less likely to lose the basic idea of the sentence through improper synthesis. Similarly, if relatively complex phrases and clauses within a single sentence are replaced by shorter separate sentences, 🙂 would be less likely to lose track of where the sentence is going. Wiener and his associates have conducted a series of research studies that give general support to these conclusions.

Finally, an internal technique might be employed with 😐 , also a student with *difference* problems. For example, as mentioned in Chapter 4, I have found in my own research that certain poor readers (specifically those with synthesis problems) are often able to improve their reading comprehension if they simply attempt to develop a clear picture in their minds of the information contained in each sentence of a reading passage. Moreover, this strategy seems to benefit students with other types of learning difficulties as well (Levin, 1976). The long-term benefits associated with strategies such as this still need to be investigated.

Steps 5 and 6: Action and Assessment

There is little that needs to be said about the two final steps of the Figure 2.5 model. As we noted in Chapter 4, our prescriptions will not always work because of individual differences in responsiveness to particular instructional treatments. Thus, for the unmotivated child, the chief task might consist of searching for an appropriate incentive; for the child who is easily distracted, it might consist of searching for the right information-dissemination mode or medium; and so on.

Concluding Remarks

In spite of the fact that there are no guarantees for success, we must persist in individualizing instruction for as many students as possible. To do this, we must continue to view students as individuals. Our classrooms are full not of "average" students but of individuals, each with his or her own aptitudes and abilities, and other distinctive learner characteristics. If our goal is to maximize output, we must be aware of those differences and attempt to deal with them in a rational manner. Only then will we be taking a serious crack at the cherished chestnut that we have been referring to as "learner differences."

Suggested Readings

Baer, D. M. *Student motivation and behavior modification*. New York: Holt, Rinehart and Winston, forthcoming.

Gagné, R. M. *Essentials of learning for instruction*. New York, Holt, Rinehart and Winston, 1974.

Wiener, M., & Cromer, W. Reading and reading difficulty: A conceptual analysis. *Harvard Educational Review*, 1967, **37**, 620–643.

References

Ammon, P. R. The cognitive approach to intellectual development. In W. D. Rohwer, Jr., P. R. Ammon, & P. Cramer. *Understanding intellectual development.* New York: Holt, Rinehart and Winston, 1974.

Anastasi, A. *Differential psychology.* New York: Macmillan, 1958.

Atkinson, R. C., & Wilson, H. A. (Eds.) *Computer-assisted instruction: A book of readings.* New York: Academic Press, 1969.

Baer, D. M. *Student motivation and behavior modification.* New York: Holt, Rinehart and Winston, forthcoming.

Baltes, P. B., & Schaie, K. W. Aging and IQ: The

myth of the twilight years. *Psychology Today*, 1974, **7**, 35–40.

Bender, N. N. Self-verbalization versus tutor verbalization in modifying impulsivity. *Journal of Educational Psychology*, 1976, **68**, 347–354.

Berliner, D. C., & Cahen, L. S. Trait-treatment interaction and learning. In F. N. Kerlinger (Ed.), *Review of research in education*, Vol. 1. Itasca, Ill.: Peacock, 1973.

Bissell, J., White, S., & Zivin, G. Sensory modalities in children's learning. In G. S. Lesser (Ed.), *Psychology and educational practice*. Glenview, Ill.: Scott, Foresman and Co., 1971.

Brophy, J. E., & Good, T. L. *Teacher-student relationships: Causes and consequences.* New York: Holt, Rinehart and Winston, 1974.

Brown, A. L. The role of strategic behavior in retardate memory. In N. R. Ellis (Ed.), *International Review of Research in Mental Retardation* (Vol. 7). New York: Academic Press, 1974.

Bruner, J. S. *The process of education.* New York: Vintage, 1960.

Bruner, J. S., Olver, R. R., & Greenfield, P. M., et al. *Studies in cognitive growth.* New York: John Wiley & Sons, 1966.

Buros, O. K. (Ed.) *The seventh mental measurements yearbook.* Vols. I and II. Highland Park, N.J.: Gryphon, 1972.

Carroll, J. A model of school learning. *Teachers College Record*, 1963, **64**, 723–733.

Chernoff, H. The use of faces to represent points in k-dimensional space graphically. *Journal of the American Statistical Association*, 1973, **68**, 361–368.

Coleman, J. S., et al. *Equality of educational oppor-*

tunity. Washington, D.C.: U.S. Government Printing Office, 1966.

Cook, T. D. The potential and limitations of secondary evaluation. In M. W. Apple, M. J. Subkoviak, & H. S. Lufler, Jr., (Eds.), *Educational evaluation: Analysis and responsibility*, Berkeley, Cal.: McCutchan, 1974.

Cooley, W. W., & Glaser, R. An information and management system for individually prescribed instruction. In R. C. Atkinson and H. A. Wilson (Eds.), *Computer-assisted instruction: A book of readings*. New York: Academic Press, 1969.

Cronbach, L. J. How can instruction be adapted to individual differences? In R. M. Gagné (Ed.), *Learning and individual differences*. Columbus, Ohio: Merrill, 1967.

Cronbach, L. J., & Snow, R. E. *Individual differences in learning ability as a function of instructional variables*. Final Report, March, 1969, Contract No. OEC4-6-061269-1217, U.S. Office of Education.

Cronbach, L. J., & Snow, R. E. *Aptitudes and instructional methods: A handbook for research on interactions*. New York: Irvington/Naiburg, 1976.

Dale, P. S. *Language development: Structure and function*. New York: Holt, Rinehart and Winston, 1972.

Day, H. I., & Berlyne, D. E. Intrinsic motivation. In G. S. Lesser (Ed.), *Psychology and educational practice*. Glenview, Ill.: Scott, Foresman and Co., 1971.

de Charms, R. From pawns to origins. Toward self-motivation. In G. S. Lesser (Ed.), *Psychology and educational practice*. Glenview, Ill.: Scott, Foresman and Co., 1971.

Elashoff, J. D., & Snow, R. E. *Pygmalion reconsidered*. Belmont, Cal.: Wadsworth, 1971.

Fader, D. N., & McNeil, E. B. *Hooked on books: Program & proof*. New York: Berkeley, 1968.

Farnham-Diggory, S. Symbol and synthesis in experimental reading. *Child Development*, 1967, **38**, 223–231.

Fuller, R. Breaking down the IQ walls: Severely retarded people *can* learn to read. *Psychology Today*, 1974, **8**, 96–102.

Furth, H. G. *Piaget for teachers*. Englewood Cliffs, N.J.: Prentice-Hall, 1970.

Gage, N. L., & Unruh, W. R. Theoretical formulations for research on teaching. *Review of Educational Research*, 1967, **37**, 358–370.

Gagné, R. M. *Essentials of learning for instruction*. New York: Holt, Rinehart and Winston, 1974.

Gaite, A. J. H. Preschool play behavior: Then and now. *Instructor*, 1974, **84**, 36.

Ginsburg, H. & Opper, S. *Piaget's theory of intellectual development: An introduction*. Englewood Cliffs, N.J.: Prentice-Hall, 1969.

Glaser, R. Individuals and learning: The new aptitudes. *Educational Researcher*, 1972, **1** (6), 5–13.

Green, D. R. *Evaluating instruction*. New York: Holt, Rinehart and Winston, forthcoming.

Grubb, R. E. Learner-controlled statistics. In R. C. Atkinson & H. A. Wilson (Eds.), *Computer-assisted instruction: A book of readings*. New York: Academic Press, 1969.

Hambleton, R. K. Testing and decision-making procedures for selected individualized instructional programs. *Review of Educational Research*, 1974, **44**, 371–400.

Hunt, J. McV. *Intelligence and experience*. New York: Ronald Press, 1961.

Ingison, L. J., & Levin, J. R. The effect of children's

spontaneous cognitive sets on discrimination learning. *Journal of Experimental Child Psychology*, 1975, **20**, 59–65.

Jensen, A. R. How much can we boost IQ and scholastic achievement? *Harvard Educational Review*, 1969, **39**, 1–123.

Kagan, J., Moss, H. A., & Sigel, I. E. Psychological significance of styles of conceptualization. *Monograph of the Society for Research in Child Development*, 1963, **28**, 73–111.

Karier, C. J. Ideology and evaluation: In quest of meritocracy. In M. W. Apple, M. J. Subkoviak, & H. S. Lufler, Jr. (Eds.), *Educational evaluation: Analysis and responsibility*, Berkeley, Cal.: McCutchan, 1974.

Klausmeier, H. J. The multi-unit elementary school and individually guided education. *Phi Delta Kappan*, Nov. 1971, 181–184.

Klausmeier, H. J., Jeter, J. T., Quilling, M. R., Frayer, D. A. & Allen, P. S. *Individually guided motivation* (3rd ed.). Madison: Wisconsin Research and Development Center for Cognitive Learning, 1975.

Kogan, N. Educational implications of cognitive styles. In G. S. Lesser (Ed.), *Psychology and educational practice*, Glenview, Ill.: Scott, Foresman and Co., 1971.

Kohl, H. R. *The open classroom*. New York: Vintage, 1969.

Kohlberg, L. Early education: A cognitive-developmental view. *Child Development*, 1968, **39**, 1013–1062.

Kohlberg, L., & Turiel, E. Moral development and moral education. In G. S. Lesser (Ed.), *Psychology and educational practice*. Glenview, Ill.: Scott, Foresman and Co., 1971.

Kreutzer, M. A., Leonard, Sr. C., & Flavell, J. H. An interview study of children's knowledge about memory.

Monograph of the Society for Research in Child Development, 1975, **40** (1, Serial No. 159).

Lesser, G. S. Matching instruction to student characteristics. In G. S. Lesser (Ed.), *Psychology and educational practice*. Glenview, Ill.: Scott, Foresman and Co., 1971a.

Lesser, G. S. (Ed.) *Psychology and educational practice*. Glenview, Ill.: Scott, Foresman, and Co., 1971b.

Levin, J. R. Comprehending what we read: An outsider looks in. *Journal of Reading Behavior*, 1972, **4**, 18–28.

Levin, J. R. What have we learned about maximizing what children learn? In J. R. Levin & V. L. Allen (Eds.), *Cognitive learning in children: Theories and strategies*. New York: Academic Press, 1976.

Lundsteen, S. W. *Listening: Its impact on reading and the other language arts*. Urbana, Ill.: National Council of Teachers of English, 1971.

Lyman, H. B. *Test scores and what they mean*. Englewood Cliffs, N.J.: Prentice-Hall, 1971.

McNamee, G. E. Institutional stereotypes and educational practice. In G. S. Lesser (Ed.), *Psychology and educational practice*. Glenview, Ill.: Scott, Foresman and Co., 1971.

Neill, A. S. *Summerhill: A radical approach to child rearing*. New York: Hart, 1960.

Pask, G., & Scott, B. C. E. Learning strategies and individual competence. *International Journal of Man-Machine Studies*, 1972, **4**, 217–253.

Race, intelligence and genetics. In *Psychology Today*, 1973, **7**, 79–101 (articles by A. R. Jensen, B. Rice, and T. Dobzhansky).

Ramirez, M. III, & Casteñada, A. *Cultural democracy, bicognitive development, and education*. New York:

Academic Press, 1974.

Reese, H. W. Cohort, age, and imagery in children's paired-associate learning. *Child Development*, 1974, **45**, 1176–1178.

Reese, H. W. *Basic learning processes in childhood.* New York: Holt, Rinehart and Winston, 1976.

Reese, H. W., & Lipsitt, L. P. *Experimental child psychology.* New York: Academic Press, 1970.

Rohwer, W. D., Jr. Decisive research: A means for answering fundamental questions about instruction. *Educational Researcher*, 1972, **1** (7), 5–11.

Rohwer, W. D., Jr., Ammon, P. R., & Cramer, P. *Understanding intellectual development.* New York: Holt, Rinehart and Winston, 1974.

Rosenthal, R. Teacher expectations and their effects upon children. In G. S. Lesser (Ed.), *Psychology and educational practice.* Glenview, Ill.: Scott, Foresman and Co., 1971.

Rosenthal, R., & Jacobson, L. *Pygmalion in the classroom.* New York: Holt, Rinehart and Winston, 1968.

Schmuck, R. A. Influence of the peer group. In G. S. Lesser (Ed.), *Psychology and educational practice.* Glenview, Ill.: Scott, Foresman and Co., 1971.

Shaw, M. E., & Wright, J. M. *Scales for the measurement of attitudes.* New York: McGraw-Hill, 1967.

Skinner, B. F. *The technology of teaching.* New York: Appleton-Century-Crofts, 1968.

Stanley, J. C., & Hopkins, K. D. *Educational and psychological measurement and evaluation.* Englewood Cliffs, N.J.: Prentice-Hall, 1972.

Torrance, E. P. Creativity in the educational process. In G. S. Lesser (Ed.), *Psychology and educational practice.* Glenview, Ill.: Scott, Foresman and Co., 1971.

Tyler, L. E. (Ed.) *Intelligence: Some recurring issues.*

New York: Van Nostrand Reinhold, 1969.

Tyler, L. E. *The psychology of human differences.* New York: Appleton-Century-Crofts, 1965.

Waynant, L. F., & Wilson, R. M. *Learning centers . . . A guide for effective use.* Paoli, Penn.: Instructo Corp., 1974.

Wiener, M., & Cromer, W. Reading and reading difficulty: A conceptual analysis. *Harvard Educational Review,* 1967, **37**, 620–643.

Witkin, H. A. *The role of cognitive style in academic performance and in teacher-student relations.* Research Bulletin #73-11. Princeton, N.J.: Educational Testing Service, 1973.

Ysseldyke, J. E. Diagnostic-prescriptive teaching: The search for aptitude-treatment interactions. In L. Mann & D. A. Sabatino (Eds.), *The first review of special education.* Philadelphia: JSE Press, 1973.

Yussen, S. R., Levin, J. R., DeRose, T. M., & Ghatala, E. S. Individual differences in young children's recall and clustering of pictures. *Contemporary Educational Psychology,* 1976, **1**, 170–179.

Index